The

NORTHERN ROCKIES

A Touring Guide

Idaho, Montana,
Wyoming, Black Hills &
Black Hills of South Dakota

The

NORTHERN ROCKIES

A Touring Guide

*Idaho, Montana,
Wyoming, Black Hills &
Black Hills of South Dakota*

Larry H. Ludmer

HUNTER
PUBLISHING INC

Hunter Publishing, Inc.
300 Raritan Center Parkway
Edison NJ 08818
Tel (908) 225 1900
Fax (908) 417 0482

ISBN 1-55650-684-8

Maps by Kim André

Cover Photograph:
Castle Geyser, Yellowstone National Park
Superstock

Contents

Maps

Introduction

This is the second in a series of touring guides that will, upon completion, be a concise and useful collection of sightseeing companions for the American traveler. The first book in the series, *Arizona, Utah & Colorado: A Touring Guide*, covered the major portion of the southern Rocky Mountain states. This volume tours the northern Rockies in separate trips to Wyoming (along with the southwestern corner of South Dakota), Montana and Idaho. While still dominated by the Rocky Mountains, these states are clearly different from their neighbors to the south. There are no big cities and no urban congestion here – only wide-open spaces and small cities (large towns would generally be a more appropriate description) that reflect a slower pace of life and a greater appreciation for the beauty of the surrounding countryside. But you'll find more than scenery, for everywhere that you travel will bring you in touch with the region's exciting history, from Native Americans to explorers to cowboys. It's a combination that adds color and fun to the majestic sights that will surround you throughout your journey.

Nowhere is the history of the American West more in evidence than in Wyoming, a state that is so associated with "cowboys" that a bronco-busting hero adorns the license plate of every Wyoming vehicle. *America the Beautiful* seems to have been written about this landscape. Above all, however, people think of Yellowstone when they think of Wyoming. And no wonder. Perhaps nowhere else in all the world is the diversity of nature represented in so relatively small an area. Unusual geologic wonders, so common in Yellowstone are also found in the unique Badlands and Black Hills of South Dakota.

The contrasts of Montana are equally impressive. From endless high plains in the eastern portion of the state to some of the most magnificent mountain scenery found anywhere, Montana well deserves the name "Big Sky Country," even though the official nickname is the less colorful "Treasure State."

Mountains, lakes and forests, as well as unusual geologic formations cover the length and breadth of Idaho, which we refer to as the "secret beauty" because it is far less visited than many other areas of the American West. That is both a good and bad thing. Good because it helps to preserve the beauty of the state, which can be both rugged and gentle, in a pristine condition; but bad because its sights should be seen by everyone.

The states in this guide are linked by the common thread of the Rockies and by history. Whether you visit only one at length, take in a bit of each, or go for an extended journey through all of them, you will come away with a greater love of the beauty of nature, a new understanding of their "cowboy and Indian" history, and a wish to return again and again.

Getting Started

The chapters that describe the sights of Wyoming, Montana, and Idaho are arranged in three roughly circular routes, one for each state (with the southwestern portion of South Dakota included in the Wyoming chapter). Each route covers dozens of major attractions, including some of America's most famous national parks, as well as many smaller, lesser known places to visit. The suggested itineraries are all similar in their mileage. The basic Wyoming and Montana trips are approximately 1,650 miles each, while Idaho is about 150 miles shorter. These distances are exclusive of any alternative routes or side trips that you may add.

You are not limited to the suggested routes, however. Information on deviating from the route will be given in the final portion of each chapter. The purpose of the circle route is to provide a framework for your trip. You may want to condense it, lengthen it, or simply stray from the outline here and there.

Between the main route and the alternatives provided to add to or replace parts of the primary route, you'll be able to cover virtually every part of these three states. But do keep in mind that, unless you're on an extended journey, it's simply not possible to see all that each of these large states has to offer in a single trip.

Any visit to the Northern Rocky Mountain states will, of course, focus on scenic attractions. But we won't ignore the history buff either. Even the small cities of the region offer plenty of interesting things to see and do – often much more in relationship to their size than you would imagine. Let's take a look at some practical considerations before we begin our journey.

When to Go

All of the states in this guide have a lot for the winter sports enthusiast. Idaho's Sun Valley, for instance, is one of America's best skiing locations. The beauty of the mountains in winter, covered with a blanket of snow, is a most inspiring sight. On the other hand, extreme cold, impassable mountain roads, and reduced hours of operation at various historic attractions (if they're open at all), make winter a poor choice for visiting the area unless you're here to ski.

The northern Rockies are simply delightful during the summer. Days are dominated by an abundance of sunshine, usually broken only by afternoon thunderstorms. Long periods of bad weather are unusual at this time of year. Despite the amount of sun, temperatures are generally comfortable, even cool in the higher mountain elevations. Some of the cities in valley areas can get hot – well into the 90s on many occasions, but the air is usually so dry that even the high temperatures can be well tolerated by most people. Regardless of where in the region you travel, though, evenings are often brisk and a jacket or sweater is essential.

Summer is the most crowded time of the year as far as visitors are concerned. While that may be a minor drawback, it shouldn't deter you from considering the period from June through Labor Day as the time to go. While the weather in the late spring and early fall is usually quite nice, it can often be a bit on the cool side for outdoor activities. More important, some mountain roads don't open before the summer and you could find yourself caught in a late spring or early fall snowstorm. Although they aren't necessarily the rule, they can and do happen. Normal temperature ranges and rainfall amounts (in inches) for selected locations are listed in the chart below:

	JANUARY High/Low/Rain	APRIL High/Low/Rain	JULY High/Low/Rain	OCTOBER High/Low/Rain
Cheyenne	38/14/0.6	55/29/2.1	84/54/2.0	62/33/1.1
Yellowstone	26/10/0.9	48/26/2.5	76/47/2.7	52/29/1.6
Rapid City	34/10/0.5	57/32/2.0	88/60/2.1	63/37/1.1
Billings	33/13/0.5	57/34/1.0	89/58/1.1	63/37/1.1
Great Falls	32/14/0.6	55/33/0.9	84/56/1.3	59/38/0.7
Boise	36/21/1.3	62/37/1.1	90/59/0.2	65/40/0.9
Idaho Falls	28/03/1.8	58/29/2.0	88/50/0.9	62/28/1.5

You should pack clothes appropriate to the season, keeping in mind that a jacket is always a necessary item even in the middle of summer. It is best to dress in layers in all seasons so that you can adjust to the large daily temperature range here. Just as important is to remember to pack light. Unless you're going to be staying at a fancy resort (few and far between in these parts), you'll find this to be a most casual area. Even most of the best restaurants don't require that you dress up for dinner. This is outdoor country so dress for it and be comfortable.

The itineraries in this book assume that you will be traveling during the summer. If not, be sure to verify operating hours (the hours shown in the Quick Reference Attraction Index are for the summer months).

Time Allotment

No two people want to spend the same amount of time seeing a given list of attractions. It's certainly not the intention of this guide to dictate a style to you – do what you're comfortable with. However, we do suggest a time frame for each of the primary itineraries that is approximately 12 days long and is based on several assumptions, including the following.

- Limiting driving to a *maximum* of about 250 miles per day, with the average mileage being a very manageable 140 per day.

- An activity day beginning around eight in the morning and ending at about five in the afternoon.

- A brief stop for lunch.

- Sightseeing times at each attraction as described in the chapters that follow. If no mention of time is made for a particular attraction it means that the majority of visitors will spend under a half-hour at that location. Hours of operation can be found in the Quick Reference Attraction Index (Addendum 2).

Although many miles of driving will be done on fast Interstate highways, this part of the country is dominated by slower roads, often of a narrow and winding nature. In calculating driving time, never assume that you can average more than 40 miles per hour when not on an Interstate highway.

Lodging and Dining

Many travel guides devote much space to detailed descriptions of a few places to stay or a few restaurants and act as if those are the only choices you have. We don't propose to dictate to the reader in this manner. Our objective is to help you decide by informing you as to where accommodations can be found, but not to decide for you. This book will provide information on areas to seek out that have the greatest variety in lodging and dining along your route so that you'll be able to find something that suits your tastes and budget. In addition, Addendum 3 offers a list indicating where major chain hotels can be found in each state. We'll also give you telephone numbers that you can call to get complete directory information for virtually all of the major chains. Additional sources of places to stay and eat can be found in the appropriate state or regional **AAA TourBooks** or **Mobil Travel Guides**. State tourism offices also will send you information on lodging and dining facilities.

Pre-Planned vs. Day-to-Day Approach

There are two possible approaches to any sightseeing trip. The first is to carefully plan each day, allocating a certain amount of time for traveling, seeing the various attractions along the way, and then ending the day in a predetermined place with a room booked in advance. Or you can take things as they come, spending as little or as much time in each place as you want to and, when you've had enough at the end of the day, find a place to spend the night. When you have a pre-planned itinerary you can be reasonably certain that you will accomplish most of what you set out to do. This is important if you have a limited amount of vacation time and want to get the most out of it. By making hotel reservations in advance you won't waste time looking for a place to stay or be confronted by "No Vacancy" signs. The latter can be a real problem in out-of-the-way places where rooms are few and are quickly gobbled up by tour groups. The primary advantage of the day-to-day approach is its flexibility. Enjoying a particular place? Then stay a little (or a lot) longer. For many travelers the planning stage is fun – it whets the appetite for the real thing. Others have difficulty in figuring out an itinerary or how much time to allot for this or that. If you are good at planning, or even if you aren't, this book will provide the means for developing a successful plan, whether you follow the main suggested route to the letter or use it as a base to work from.

You can combine the two approaches to some degree and here's how to do it. Decide where you want to spend each night based on the amount of mileage you want to cover each day. Don't allocate a specific amount of time for each attraction on the route that day. Instead, use the ad hoc approach. There is some risk that you'll run out of time on any given day but, if you do, you'll still have spent the most time at those attractions that you enjoy. On the other hand, if nothing appeals to you early in the day, you can almost always find something to add on, so you won't risk reaching your destination at two o'clock in the afternoon with nothing else to do.

Some Final Words of Wisdom

The suggested itineraries begin in Cheyenne, Billings, and Boise, respectively, for each of the three trips. If you're flying to your starting point and renting a car, these are the logical choices because convenient air connections can be made to each of them (direct flights are probably not available unless you live in a major western air hub such as Denver or Salt Lake City). A variety of car rental agencies can be found at or near the three airports. (Each itinerary will also provide an alternative "flying" gateway that allows for a wider choice of flights from anywhere in the country, but may require more driving to reach the main route.)

If you're taking a "fly/drive" trip remember that the lowest airline fares apply to round-trip flights. Similarly, car rentals are less expensive if you return your vehicle to the same location. One-way drop-off fees are often expensive, if the privilege is offered at all. Local car rental companies frequently have lower rates than the major national chains.

For those of you who drive here, plan on joining the route at the *closest* point. There is no reason to waste time and gas getting to "Point A" just because we've made it our starting point.

No matter how carefully you plan, there is always a good chance you will get lost at some point. The three state maps in this book are schematic representations of the suggested and alternative sightseeing routes that provide an overall picture of your trip. Do not rely on them to find your way around. Bring a map of each state that you will be visiting (AAA maps are among the best, but official highway maps available from each state's tourism office are also excellent). These should be supplemented with detailed city maps if you're going to be straying off the highways in larger urban areas and by maps of the National Parks that are available from the Park Service. Information on contacting these sources is available in Addendum 3. We're now ready to begin our journey!

Chapter 1

Wyoming
Land of Contrasts

Including South Dakota's Badlands and Black Hills

Wyoming is the home to two of America's most outstanding National Parks – Yellowstone and Grand Teton. They sit one atop the other in the northwestern corner of this large, rectangular-shaped state. While they may be the highlight of any Wyoming visit, they represent only a small part of the state and, likewise, only a portion of the many wonderful attractions that await you. A trip across Wyoming will bring you face to face with scenery ranging from alpine forests to landscapes that appear almost unearthly. Here, too, is found the spirit that made the American West what it is – individualistic, for sure, but progressive as well, for Wyoming was, among other things, the first to grant women the right to vote (back in 1869). The southwestern corner of South Dakota is included in this trip for reasons explained later. It contains some of the most unusual and beautiful scenery in all of the West. The attractions covered are within a reasonable distance of the Wyoming state line and make for an unforgettable adventure.

Along the Suggested Itinerary

We'll begin our tour in the state capital of Cheyenne. Easy connections by air can be made to and from most western cities. If you prefer, you can fly into Denver and travel along Interstate 25 north directly into Cheyenne. The one-way distance is almost 100 miles and can be accomplished in well under two hours. Flights to Jackson, near Grand Teton and Yellowstone National Parks, are readily available and provide another possible starting point, although we don't usually like to begin the trip with what may be the best part. For those readers arriving by car, there are several gateways into Wyoming. Interstate 80 runs along the entire southern section of the state, while Interstate 90 traverses the northeastern portion. Those coming from the south will be using I-25. A brief look at the accompanying map will clearly show the routes to the nearest intersecting point of the suggested itinerary.

With a population of about 50,000, Cheyenne is one of the smallest of America's state capitals. At an altitude of just over 6,000 feet, it's also the highest, topping Denver's mile-high status. Getting around a town of this size doesn't present any problems. Interstates 25 and 80 form an "L" along Cheyenne's western and southern boundaries, while US Routes 30 (east-west) and 85 (north-south) are the main arteries within the city itself. The terminal for Cheyenne Municipal Airport is right off of US 85 and is only a mile from downtown via Central Avenue.

The best place to begin touring is in the heart of the city – the capitol complex. The **Wyoming State Capitol** (Capitol Avenue between 24th and 25th Streets) is a traditional classic design for a very untraditional state. The dark sandstone exterior is surmounted by a beautiful golden dome that measures 50 feet in diameter. Exhibits pertaining to various aspects of the state's natural resources adorn the interior. Don't miss the lifelike bronco-busting cowboy statue on the grounds. This large bronze work captures the frontier spirit that remains a strong part of the Wyoming way of life as we approach the 21st century. The **Wyoming State Museum**, across the street from the Capitol at 24th and Central, uses both documents and exhibits to portray the state's colorful history. Allow at least 90 minutes to tour the entire capitol complex.

At 300 East 21st Street is the **Historic Governors' Mansion State Historic Site**. The colonial-style mansion was home to the governor until as recently as 1976. Your visit begins with a video describing some of the building's more interesting occupants as well as its design. It was constructed in 1904. Approximately 45 minutes is needed to see the house.

The **Cheyenne Frontier Days Old West Museum,** located in Lions Park north of downtown at N. Carey Avenue and 8th Street, is Cheyenne's highlight for many visitors. The museum houses several displays that depict important aspects of area history, including exhibits on the Sioux Indians and the Union Pacific Railroad. Lions Park, a large and attractive urban park, is a good spot to relax when you get tired of sightseeing. At least 45 minutes is needed to see the museum in full.

If you have only a short time in Cheyenne, take the two-hour sightseeing tour on the **Cheyenne Street Railway Trolley**, departing from near the Capitol at Lincolnway and Capitol Avenue.

Although Cheyenne may be Wyoming's "Metropolis," don't expect anything resembling a large city. It's a nice town with dozens of places to stay, including nearly all of the major chains. Holding's Little America Hotel is the finest and most famous lodging establishment in Cheyenne and even has gourmet continental dining. Otherwise, things tend to be simple here, making it a great introduction to a very informal state. The Frontier Mall does have about 75 stores for habitual shoppers. If you happen to be here in the final week of July, a special treat is in store for you. **Cheyenne Frontier Days**, one of the nation's largest rodeos and Wild West celebrations, takes place at the Frontier Park Rodeo Grounds in Lions Park with related events all over town. Almost the entire population of Cheyenne gets involved and it's a fun time for all. Things get pretty crowded so if you do plan to partake, make lodging reservations well in advance.

Leave Cheyenne via I-25, heading north for approximately 70 miles to the town of Wheatland. As the name implies, the growing of wheat has, and continues to be, the primary business activity here. The **Laramie Peak Museum** has artifacts relating to the history of the region, including the town's importance as part of the Oregon Trail. Continue on I-25 for another 55 miles to Exit 135 and the town of Douglas.

Douglas may not be as familiar to people as many of the West's notorious cowboy frontier towns, such as Tombstone or Dodge City, but it has as wild a history. Some of its rowdy and colorful past comes alive at the **Wyoming Pioneer Memorial Museum**, located on the state fairgrounds in town. Set on the scenic North Platte River, Douglas provides ample opportunity for strolling and biking, as well as nature walks on the **Scenic River Path**, which runs for about 2½ miles along the river through downtown.

From the center of town head northwest following the signs for **Fort Fetterman State Historic Site**. Here you'll encounter a living history museum in the form of an 1867 army frontier supply post. The officers' quarters and other buildings have been restored to their original appearance and a museum displays uniforms and weapons. Allow at least an hour to visit the site and more if you come during Fort Fetterman Days in July when reenactment festivities are staged.

Ayres Natural Bridge, 12 miles west of Douglas via I-25 then south on Natural Bridge Road, is a 30-foot-high natural stone bridge carved by the creek below. It doesn't seem possible that this small river could have cut a 50-foot-wide hole through solid rock, but it has. Evidence indicates that the creek was once more forceful than it is today.

Return to I-25 northbound and continue towards Casper. A brief stop can be made in the town of Glenrock, about half-way between Douglas and Casper. The town is named for a large rock formation that was a conspicuous landmark on the Oregon Trail. The wagon ruts from over 100 years ago are still clearly visible.

Casper, a few thousand people smaller than Cheyenne, is Wyoming's second largest community. It, too, began as a stop on the many trails used by settlers heading west. The town only really started to grow in 1889 when oil was discovered nearby, an industry which still is of great importance to the local economy. An interesting side trip towards the southwest is available from Casper and is described in the last section of this chapter. (Rodeo is popular here, too, and the biggest one is held at the end of July through early August).

Fort Caspar Museum (not a misspelling, the town uses an "e"), was named for Caspar Collins, a young army officer who was killed while trying to save a wagon train from an Indian attack. The museum recreates a fort that once existed here and displays both pioneer and Indian relics. Good views of Casper and the surrounding area can be had at the top of **Casper Mountain Park**, about 10 miles south of downtown via SR 251, also known as Casper Mountain Road. Casper provides a good selection of accommodations and dining options, most at very moderate prices (except during fairs when prices are higher).

Upon leaving Casper via I-25, take Exit 189 onto US 20 and US 26 west. Some 40 miles west of Casper, just beyond the small town of Powder River, is one of Wyoming's most unusual attractions – **Hell's Half Acre**. The name is totally innacurate when it comes to math, since the area covers a much larger 320 acres. The site is a marvel of nature. Erosion has created a glorious array of shapes among the rocks in this natural depression. It is referred to by

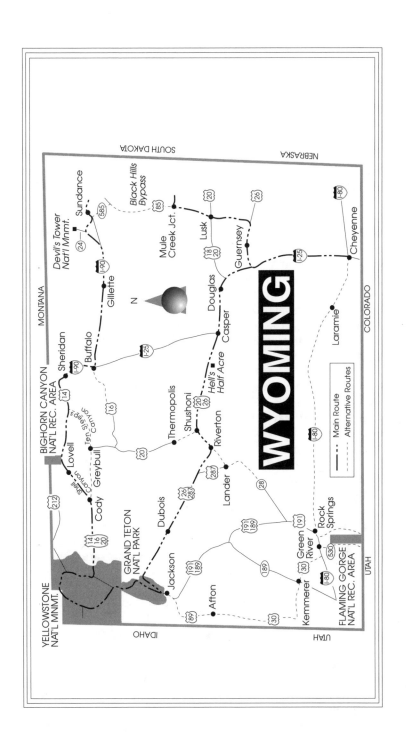

some as the "Baby Grand Canyon," although there is more resemblance to Bryce or similar geologic oddities often found in Utah. In any event, the strange formations are made all the more beautiful (or eerie, depending upon your point of view) by the variety of delicate colors that shade through them. Archaeologists believe that native Americans once used this maze-like terrain for trapping buffalo. Allow close to an hour for your visit.

From Hell's Half Acre continue west on US 20/26 until Shoshone (55 miles) where the two roads split. Stay on US 26 (a side trip continuing along US 20 is described later) for 22 more miles until the town of Riverton. The last 10 miles of this journey are traveling on the Wind River Indian Reservation, the largest reservation in the state of Wyoming. The **Riverton Museum** has exhibits on the Shoshone and Arapaho Indians, as well as a reconstructed pioneer town. The museum is more extensive than many others of this genre and a good visit requires between 45 minutes and an hour. Riverton, the first significant town you'll have encountered since leaving Casper, is a good place to stay overnight. A side trip continuing south from Riverton into the Lower Wind River Basin is discussed later.

For now you'll continue west on US 26, which in a little more than a half-hour joins US 287 (northbound). Dubois is located between where the road leaves the Wind River Reservation and enters a series of contiguous National Forest lands beginning with the Shoshone National Forest. The road to Dubois is quite scenic, as it parallels a long stretch of the Continental Divide. Included among the sights are Gannett Peak, Wyoming's highest point at 13,804 feet. In the town itself is the **Dubois Museum**, an interesting local area history museum, and the far more interesting **National Bighorn Sheep Interpretive Center**. Somewhere in your trip through Wyoming you're bound to see bighorn sheep in the wild. These most impressive and beautiful animals are commonly sighted along mountain slopes and rocky crevices. If you're not that fortunate, however, you'll find out a lot about them at the Interpretive Center, which uses mounted specimens and dioramas to inform visitors about these creatures. There is even an artificial sheep mountain that shows the relationship of bighorn sheep to the animals and vegetation around them. Allow about 45 minutes to explore the center.

One other attraction near town is the **Dubois Fish Hatchery**, located three miles east of town, then by a short access road. Several varieties of trout are raised here and you can see some of the more than 7 million fish that the hatchery produces each year. A number of motels are located in town, including a member of the budget Super 8 motel chain.

Thirty miles west of Dubois, still on US 26/287, you'll cross the Continental Divide at the Togwotee Pass. The area is known primarily for winter sports, but there isn't any rule prohibiting summer visitors from enjoying the view. The road winds in and out and has some fairly steep grades in parts, but presents no driving problems. After the pass you enter the beautiful Bridger-Teton National Forest for the descent towards Moran Junction and Grand Teton National Park. One of the most picturesque attractions near the road is the area around **Brooks Lake**. This alpine lake lies at an elevation of more than 9,000 feet and is backed by towering granite peaks.

It's hardly possible to ignore Grand Teton, but we'll do so for the moment as we explore it later on during this tour. At Moran Junction, where several US highway routes converge, head south on US 26/89/191 for 31 miles to the town of Jackson, sometimes called Jackson Hole because of its location in one of the broadest and most spectacular valleys in the nation. There are many things to do and see in this town that lies at the southern end of the National Park, and we'll describe them before sending you on to explore Grand Teton itself.

Jackson is one of Wyoming's biggest tourist towns, so there is a wide choice of lodging and dining establishments. This town of 4,500 people has no fewer than three dozen motels and hotels covering every price and luxury range. Restaurants offer anything from American to Mexican and continental cuisine. For those in need of a real "Western" meal, try the Bar-J Chuckwagon Supper or the Bar-T Five Covered Wagon Cookout and Wild West Show. Each features home cookin' and Western entertainment, but the latter includes a lovely ride by covered wagon into a scenic canyon where the dinner and show are held. The entire town of Jackson is like something out of a Western theme park; even the streets feature Old West boardwalks. You can spend the evening listening to some late 19th-century-style music hall entertainment. In addition, every conceivable type of outdoor recreational activity – winter and summer – can be found in the valley of Jackson Hole.

A *must* for visitors to Jackson and Grand Teton is a float trip on the Snake River. These rides range from wild whitewater rapids south of the town in the scenic forested mountains of Bridger-Teton, to calm float trips heading north into the National Park. The more relaxing trips pass through sections of the park that are close to and parallel Grand Teton's extensive road system, but are still a highly worthwhile activity. The length of each trip varies from a couple of hours to a full day. Transportation to the launch site is provided. There are a dozen different operators, many providing nationwide toll-free numbers. See the Addendum for further information.

Within the town of Jackson itself are several interesting attractions. The **Jackson Hole Museum** features exhibits on the area's history as a fur trading center, local archaeology, and more. **Ross Berlin's Wildlife Museum** has many mounted specimens of big game animals. A more interesting part of your visit, which will take at least a half-hour, is the guided tour of the taxidermy shop. The final museum that you should stop at in Jackson is the **Wax Museum of Old Wyoming**. This fun place features "the good, the bad, and the ugly" of the Wild West with life-size costumed figures and realistic background scenes. A minimum of a half-hour should be allowed for this attraction as well.

While Jackson is a most interesting place, you come to Jackson Hole for the scenery and that can certainly be found at the next attraction – the **Jackson Hole Aerial Tram**, located less than a half-hour from town. A mile south of town take SR 22 for four miles, then head eight miles north on SR 390. The tram, set in a winter ski resort area, takes you to the top of 10,450-foot Rendezvous Mountain, a distance of almost 2½ miles from the base station. It is one of the longest tram rides in North America. From the top there is a breathtaking view of not only the majestic Teton Range, but the entire valley of Jackson Hole. Allow about an hour for the round-trip tram ride and some time at the summit. A closer alternative, the **Snow King Scenic Chairlift & Alpine Slide**, is not far from the center of town on E. Snow King Avenue. The chairlift provides excellent views and there are nature trails at the top. You can even descend the 2,500 feet back into town on the alpine slide, twisting your way through the forested mountain slope! Snow King requires between 45 minutes to an hour of your time.

For those visitors here from November through April, the **National Elk Refuge**, located only a mile east of town, is home to one of the largest herds of elk in North America. Over 7,500 of the animals make this their winter home. Unfortunately, they migrate elsewhere during the summer migration of *homo sapiens* into Wyoming.

An option for those who have time on their hands is to take one of the many multi-day (usually up to four days) trips by covered wagon that explore the Grand Teton-Yellowstone countryside. These complete packages are expensive, but they provide the opportunity to rough it without too much hardship. For information on contacting operators see the Addendum.

We're almost ready to head into Grand Teton National Park, but there's one stop on the way in. About 10 miles north of Jackson, then east following signs, is the site of the 1927 **Gros Ventre Slide** area. Now a part of the Bridger Teton National Forest, the area encompasses the remains of a large earth movement that had previously blocked up the river, then gave way. The ensuing wall of water, rock and mud completely destroyed the town of Kelly. Although nature has restored the trees on the mountainside, there remains ample evidence of the disaster. Self-guiding trails lead through the slide area. Allow about an hour.

The northwest corner of the state is home to Wyoming's two biggest attractions – Yellowstone and Grand Teton National Parks, which are separated by only five miles of the scenic John D. Rockefeller Parkway. Yellowstone is the premier attraction of Wyoming and, perhaps, the world. And if Yellowstone is the main course, then it's certainly safe to say that Grand Teton is a fitting appetizer. (It could even be the dessert if you're doing the trip in reverse!) Yet, it isn't fair to compare them, for not only is Grand Teton a world class attraction in itself, but the two parks are *completely* different in the nature of their scenery.

Grand Teton National Park begins a few hundred feet north of Jackson. It provides the best of both worlds; some of the most vigorous outdoor activities along with being a great place to relax. If you're following the suggested route, you'll have come south through the park on the Rockefeller Parkway, an excellent road that provides outstanding views of the sharply rising Teton Range. However, we won't be heading back north through the park via the same route. Moose Junction, where the Park Headquarters and main visitor center are located, is a good place to stock up on brochures and information on park activities.

The Teton Range is one of the most dramatic mountain ranges in the United States. Grand Teton itself, the largest, rises to an altitude of 13,770 feet while 10 other peaks soar higher than 11,000. The fact that the mountains rise in a sharp, almost vertical ascent from the surrounding flat valley of Jackson Hole makes them appear even higher and more beautiful. You won't have any doubts as to why they've been favorably compared with the Swiss Alps.

After the Moose Visitor Center, pick up the Teton Park Road. It parallels the Rockefeller Parkway and provides another easy drive with magnificent scenery. (It will rejoin the parkway, which is also US 89, just before Jackson Lake Lodge.) This road is closer to the base of the mountains than the Parkway and offers access to the best sights and park activities. Make use of the pullouts along the road (there are many pullouts along the Rockefeller Parkway, too) to get a better view – you'll have to be a neck contortionist to see the peaks from inside your car! The first stop, just minutes from the visitor center, should be the Chapel of the Transfiguration, a log cabin built in 1925. An open "window" at the altar end provides an unforgettable mountain vista. Shortly after this you'll reach the South Jenny Lake Junction. Frequent launch service provided by the Park Service will take you for a short ride to the far shore of the lake and the beginning of an easy trail to Hidden Falls. You'll hear the rushing water long before you can see it; in fact, you don't catch a glimpse of the falls until practically walking into them. You then have to come back the opposite way and take the launch once again.

Those who enjoy walking should try the two-mile Colter Bay Nature Trail. The Colter Bay Visitor Center here is primarily devoted to the Indian cultures that dominated the area long before its discovery by Europeans. If you happen to be in Grand Teton on a Friday evening in the summer at 8:30, you should see the colorful Laubin Ancient Indian Dancers perform at Jackson Lake Lodge. By the way, the lodge is worth a visit just to admire its handsome wooden architecture. The hotel's terrace provides some outstanding views of the mountains. While at Jenny Lake you can also take a 90-minute cruise on the largest lake in Grand Teton National Park, a very relaxing and scenic journey if you have the time to spare.

In addition to the float trips already mentioned (many leave from within Grand Teton), the more adventurous may want to see the park by horseback or actually climb one of the Tetons. They're not especially difficult to scale and lessons are given throughout the summer. A final option is the somewhat difficult five-mile unpaved spur road leading to the top of Signal Mountain. Use low gear for the entire descent. This ride affords great views from *within* the Tetons rather than looking down or up at them. An entire day should be allowed for visiting Grand Teton National Park with additional time for any serious hiking, mountain climbing and other activities. Most visitors stay overnight in Jackson as it offers a selection of hotels, but give consideration to the beautiful lodges at either Jackson Lake or Jenny Lake. Several other accommodations are available within the park confines. See the information in the Addendum.

Leaving Grand Teton by the North entrance, the Rockefeller Parkway soon brings you to the South Entrance of **Yellowstone National Park**. (There are four other access points. These are called, clockwise from the South entrance, the West, North, Northeast, and Northwest.) Yellowstone is America's first National Park, the largest outside of Alaska and probably the most diverse in its scenery. While it may be synonymous with Old Faithful to many, that and the other geysers are only one facet of this immense park that covers an area three times the size of Rhode Island! And Yellowstone has even more fascinating features to offer than Old Faithful. Despite its size, Yellowstone is one of the easiest of all National Parks to cover. Almost all the attractions lie on or near an excellent 150-mile road system called the Grand Loop Road. We'll be taking the Grand Loop in a clockwise direction, but depending upon where you enter the park you can pick it up anywhere. All of the entrance roads eventually intersect with the Grand Loop Road.

About 24 miles north of the South entrance, having climbed to the top of a forested plateau, you reach West Thumb, where one of several visitor centers in Yellowstone is located. Information on park features and activities are available here. You'll also encounter the first of many geyser basins, areas where thermal activity is present. You probably won't see any major eruptions, but the sight of steam escaping in the foreground of Yellowstone Lake is a lovely sight. The lake itself is one of the largest west of the Mississippi. A few miles later the Grand Loop crosses the Continental Divide and you'll soon reach the Old Faithful Village area. Another visitor center is here where you can check on the estimated eruption times for Old Faithful and the other active geysers. (Times are generally accurate to within a few minutes.) Be there before the eruption as crowds form rapidly and the best photo spots are quickly filled. After Old Faithful take a stroll on the trail that leads to Giant, Giantess, Castle and Grand Geysers among many others scattered along the Firehole River. The lucky ones will witness several other eruptions, but even if you only witness Old Faithful itself, the side trip along the trail is worth doing.

The Grand Loop then travels along the Firehole River, appropriately named as the hot water from steam vents running into it make it appear to be on fire. The heat along the river leads to an unusual mix of vegetation (primarily types of algae) in shades of green, red and brown. Firehole Falls is especially attractive. This area also contains the Lower and Midway Geyser Basins with their colorful "paintpots" and mud volcanos. There is the aroma of sulphur along the short trails and strange sounds coming from the earth. An important note for here and *all* areas of thermal activity: *stay on the boardwalks or designated trails.* Wandering off could be dangerous as the earth's crust is thin or hot in many places. Be certain to hold on to your children at all times!

Further north at the Norris Geyser Basin is a geology museum and, the primary attraction here, the incredible Porcelain Basin. The basin has many more of the 10,000 geysers within Yellowstone, but the biggest attention-getter here is the color – the ground is covered with algae that has combined with water and soft minerals on the surface. The result has been the creation of what looks like a giant artist's canvas with every imaginable hue. Walking through this dazzling display is unforgettable, as is the overview of the entire area that can be seen from just outside the museum. On the other side of the museum is the start of the Back Basin Trail, which contains several more very active geysers. All of these trails, as well as others we mention throughout Yellowstone, are easy. Many are almost flat and accessible to the handicapped. Check with the museum for scheduled eruption times in the Back Basin.

Continue on the Grand Loop, passing the dark and glass-like Obsidian Cliffs before reaching another of the Park's main attractions, the Mammoth Hot Springs Area. One of the larger visitor centers is located here along with the Park Headquarters. The area features multi-colored limestone terraces. Dripping water is still creating these awesome formations which are both beautiful and eerie at the same time. Boardwalks provide an almost too easy access to the most popular formations, such as the Liberty Cap, Cleopatra's Terrace, Devil's Thumb, and Minerva Terrace. In addition, there is a short one-way auto loop to the Upper Terrace.

Both terraces are generally crowded as Mammoth Springs is justifiably one of the park's most popular areas.

Upon leaving Mammoth Hot Springs the road will climb before turning south at Tower Junction. Good views of Yellowstone's highest point – Mount Washburn at 10,243 feet – are available from the road. We might add that at no point is the Grand Loop a difficult road to drive, but delays are common during heavy summer traffic. Sometimes cars are stopped so that their passengers can admire wildlife that has congregated on or adjacent to the road.

Shortly after crossing the Dunraven Pass you come to what is, in our opinion, the single most awe-inspiring section of the park – the canyon area. The remarkable Grand Canyon of The Yellowstone is a deep and spectacularly colorful gorge created by the Yellowstone River, which plunges dramatically over two falls – the 109-foot Upper Falls and the even more wonderful 300-foot Lower Falls. It is the color of the canyon's rocky walls that gives the park its name. Two short spur roads from the Canyon Village flank the north and south rims of the gorge. Each has parking areas with very short walks leading to the rim and unforgettable vistas can be had at every spot. The highlight of the south rim is the view from Artists Point, while on the north side Red Rock, Lookout Point, Grand View Point and Inspiration Point are all *must sees*. Walking trails also line the length of both rims. Misconceptions about what Yellowstone Park contains are common and uninformed visitors will be surprised by what the area has in store for them.

The Grand Loop continues south through the Hayden Valley. A stop can be made for the short trail to the Mud Volcano and other thermally active formations. Fishing Bridge and Lake Junction offer the best views of Yellowstone Lake. Before leaving Yellowstone, take a short detour south of Lake Junction to see the Natural Bridge.

Fishing Bridge is where you pick up US Routes 14, 16 and 20 eastbound to leave the park via the East entrance. Before doing so we should spend a few moments on time allocation, lodging and dining. While you can whirl through Yellowstone in one long day, that doesn't begin to do it justice. You could easily spend weeks here and not see everything. We suggest a minimum of two full days here. There are six different lodgings within the park, each of which is large, but still tends to fill up very early.

Advance reservations (see Addendum) are a must. Every facility has a restaurant or cafeteria. In addition, towns near most entrances have a variety of lodging and dining facilities, especially those at West Yellowstone (West entrance) and, to a lesser extent, Gardiner (North) and Silver Gate (Northeast). Your memory of Yellowstone will last forever. But we must, alas, draw ourselves away from this wonder of nature and continue our journey.

The three-numbered US highway extends for 52 miles from the entrance station to the town of Cody. It has been heralded as one of the most scenic roads in all of America. Traversing the Shoshone National Forest and paralleling the north fork of the Shoshone River, the route winds through the beautiful mountains and forests of Shoshone Canyon and is further highlighted by a number of unusual rock formations. The town of Cody, with 8,000 people, is an important center for agriculture and tourism. Flight-seeing, horseback riding, dude ranches and other forms of out-door recreation are all available here. In addition, if you haven't already taken a float or whitewater trip, the Cody area is an excellent place to do so as the Shoshone River is highly regarded by whitewater enthusiasts. Named for William "Buffalo Bill" Cody, the town features a statue of its namesake at the western end of Sheridan Avenue. Summer evenings feature the **Cody Nite Rodeo**, a fun event for the whole family.

The primary attractions here all relate to our Western heritage. There are four components of the **Buffalo Bill Historical Center** located in the heart of town. These consist of the Buffalo Bill Museum (about his life and times), the Cody Firearms Museum (development of firearms from the flintlock on and housing a collection of more than 5,000 pieces), the Plains Indian Museum and the Whitney Gallery of Western Art, which represents all of the major names in Western American art, including Frederick Remington. If you intend to visit all four sections, which you should if time allows, give yourself between two and three hours.

Trail Town, located two miles west of Cody, consists of several historic structures that have been brought to this site from various places in Wyoming. Allow between 30 and 45 minutes. Cody has dozens of motels, including Best Western, Comfort and Holiday Inn as well as restaurants to suit every taste.

We'll head east from Cody on Alternate US 14 (more commonly known as 14A). An alternative route described later continues on US 14/16/20 and is equally scenic. The almost 110-mile route from Cody to where it rejoins US 14/16/20 is a well-maintained road traversing beautiful mountain scenery and portions of the Bighorn National Forest. However, our primary reason for using US 14A as the main route is that it provides access to the **Bighorn Canyon National Recreation Area**, a place of outstanding beauty. Take SR 37, which begins just east of the town of Lovell, northbound into the area. The larger section of the area lies in Montana and is not accessible from the Wyoming side. However, the portion within Wyoming includes the Horseshoe Bend area that offers plenty of facilities for water sports. The lakes and rivers have been impounded by dams here. While the most spectacular section of canyon is in Montana (see next chapter), the sheer canyon walls in the south are majestic too, and need not take a back seat. The length of your visit will depend upon whether or not you're going to partake in water sports, but sightseeing should be completed in under an hour.

Returning to US 14A eastbound, the road provides access to the **Medicine Wheel**, via a fairly difficult spur road about 27 miles east of Lovell. Built by a prehistoric Indian tribe, the structure is a large circular arrangement of stones with 28 spokes. Like Stonehenge in England, Medicine Wheel is known more for what we *don't* know about it. It is believed to have had either religious or astronomical purposes. Since the road leading to Medicine Wheel isn't the best, those uncomfortable with such driving conditions may want to consider bypassing this attraction.

US 14A rejoins US 14 and then runs into I-90/US 87 about 33 miles further east. Take I-90 east to Exit 20 and the town of Sheridan. This town, rather large for Wyoming with 14,000 people, is a most interesting place, filled with Western history. Several important westward trails, most of which were very dangerous and the scene of numerous battles, are found in this region. Coal mining began in the late 19th century and remains an important part of the economy, but Sheridan truly has an Old West flavor.

In town is the **Historic Sheridan Inn**, built in 1893 and famed in its day because it contained such modern luxuries as electricity, steam heat and telephones. The inn is now a museum that describes the building's history and the lives of some of its famous and infamous guests (including Buffalo Bill, Calamity Jane and several US Presidents). The **Trail End Historic Center State Historic Site** is an elaborate mansion that was the home of US Senator John Kendrick. Guided tours lasting about 90 minutes are offered. Accommodations are available in town.

About 20 miles south of Sheridan on US 87 is the **Fetterman Massacre Monument** which commemorates the site where 82 men under the command of Col. William Fetterman were ambushed and wiped out by 2,000 Indian warriors under Chief Red Cloud in 1866. It should be noted that Col. Fetterman, like the more famous General Custer, disobeyed orders by having fewer than 100 wagons in his party. Such small parties were prone to Indian attack.

Also south of town and reached by US 87 to Big Horn is the **Bradford Brinton Memorial Museum and Historic Ranch**. It recreates 19th-century ranch life and includes a significant collection of Western art. Besides the art gallery there are about 20 rooms of the main ranch house which can be explored along with several out-buildings. Allow at least an hour for your visit. The area around Sheridan was once the home of several frontier forts. The remains of three are memorialized in the **Fort Phil Kearny State Historic Site** in Story off Exit 44 of I-90. There is a visitor center thath tells the story of the three forts and markers designating their original sites.

The town of Buffalo (follow US 87 south for one exit after it splits with I-90 at Exit 56) is another Old West town, where a stroll through "downtown" is like taking a walk into the past. The **Occidental House** is one of the community's most important structures, having served as everything from a town hall to a hospital. The **Jim Gatchell Memorial Museum** depicts local history. There is also a small amusement park called **Carousel Park**. While this may be of interest mainly to those traveling with children, others might be intrigued by its authentic 1925 carousel with beautiful hand carved wooden horses. Overnight accommodations are available in Buffalo.

Work your way back to I-90 and head eastbound for 66 miles to Exit 124 and the town of Gillette. For those interested in industrial tours, a two-hour trip through the **Amax Coal Company** can be arranged. Otherwise, a local history museum called the **Rockpile Museum** can fill up a few minutes of your time and provide a good break from the long drive on the Interstate. Continue east on I-90 to Exit 153 and take US 14 north for 26 miles to the town of Devil's Tower. From there it's six miles north on SR 24 to one of the most amazing sights in the world – **Devils Tower National Monument**.

Easily recognizable from as much as 100 miles distant, Devils Tower is a gigantic tree-stump-shaped rock rising 867 feet. It's 1,000 feet across at the base, but narrows considerably by the time it reaches the top. Devils Tower is estimated to be 50 million years old. The unusual fluted columns, which look like the pleats of an enormous drapery, have made it famous and also give it an almost delicate beauty, perhaps a strange quality in something so huge. Take a good look at it from a distance because you'll surely get a stiff neck looking up from the base.

Your visit to Devils Tower will include a stop at the visitor center and the mile-long nature trail that circles the tower. There's also a prairie dog colony within the monument and you may catch a glimpse of these furry creatures as they scurry in and out of their volcano-shaped mounds. Allow approximately two hours to visit, including a walk around the base. It's possible for experienced climbers to scale the Devils Tower and experts claim that scaling the tower isn't as difficult as it would appear. The thought scares us, but if you're into that kind of adventure ask at the visitor center.

From Devils Tower return to US 14 and continue east until arriving at the town of Sundance (motel accommodations can be found here). There is an Old West museum called the **Crook County Museum and Art Gallery**. Our suggested main route then picks up I-90 east and continues into South Dakota's Black Hills region. While we consider it an important part of the main tour, it can be bypassed if you have time limitations. If so, you can take SR 585 south from Sundance until it runs into US 85. Then head south on US 85 where it will link up with the main route once again at the town of Mule Creek Junction.

The Black Hills and Badlands of South Dakota

We include this section not only because of its geographic proximity to the eastern edge of Wyoming, but also the fact that the Black Hills and Badlands are more associated with the Rockies than the Plains of South Dakota. Whatever the reason, the sights are many and wonderful. The "hills" of the Black Hills are really mountains – the state's highest point (Mt. Haney at 7,242 feet) is in this area. But there are also thick forests, strange geological formations and plenty of history along with recreational opportunities of every kind. To make things even better, the countless attractions are all within a relatively small area – each of your stops is generally within a few minutes of the preceding one. Despite the proximity of the attractions, it can take a couple of days to see the Black Hills. There are many resorts and "tourist" towns here and finding a place to stay is not a problem. The major overnight locales are (in alphabetic order) Custer, Deadwood, Hill City, Keystone, Rapid City and Spearfish, although motels can be found in other locations as well. Restaurants can be found practically everywhere.

I-90 crosses the South Dakota line from Wyoming with your first stop only 10 miles into the state at Spearfish (Exit 10). In town is the **High Plains Heritage Center**, which has paintings and sculpture by renowned Western artists as well as a recreation of a late 1800s town. Allow between 45 minutes and an hour. Another interesting attraction in town is the **Berry Library Learning Center** on the campus of Black Hills State University. Three diverse exhibits are displayed, ranging from porcelain statues of America's first ladies, to ancient Babylonian tablets, to a gallery of wildlife art. Another 45 to 60 minutes is suggested here.

Spearfish is best known for the **Black Hills Passion Play** held in an amphitheater west of town with a mountain backdrop for the stage. The 2½-hour evening performances are held several times a week during the summer, but the grounds are open for browsing during the day. The play is, of course, similar in content to the world famous Passion Play in Germany but, thankfully (for most of us), not nearly as long.

South of Spearfish US 14A is known as the **Spearfish Canyon Scenic Highway**. It winds through the thick Black Hills National Forest. Bridal Veil Falls, located near the road, is a popular and pretty stop. The most picturesque section of the route is about 12 miles long, ending at Cheyenne Crossing where US 14A joins US 85 for the short (eight-mile) ride into the town of Lead.

Although named for the mineral, Lead is pronounced LEED. It used to be one of the largest cities in South Dakota, but its population is down to only 3,600 people these days. The **Black Hills Mining Museum** is an excellent and comprehensive presentation on the history of mining. Both educational and entertaining, the museum features a guided tour through a simulated mine. Allow at least an hour. Those wishing to see an operating gold mine can take hour-long guided tours of the famous **Homestake Gold Mine**, but the museum is, surprisingly, more interesting than the

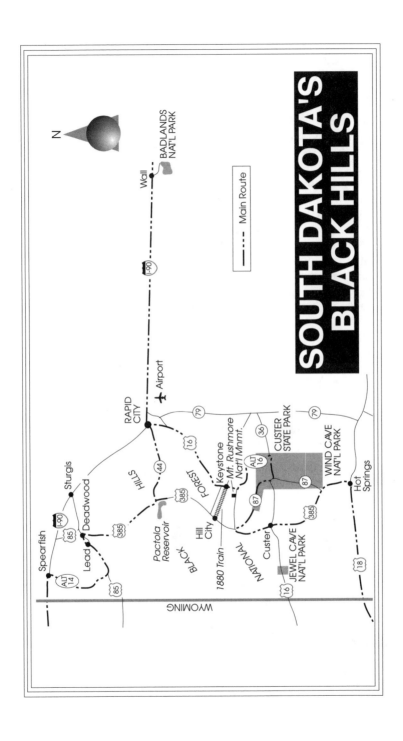

N

SOUTH DAKOTA'S
BLACK HILLS

----- Main Route

Wall

BADLANDS
NAT'L PARK

I-90

Airport

RAPID
CITY

79

Sturgis

I-90

Spearfish

85

ALT
14

Lead

Deadwood

HILLS

44

16

79

CUSTER
STATE PARK

36

Keystone

Mt. Rushmore
Nat'l Mnmt.

ALT
16

87

WIND CAVE
NAT'L PARK

87

Hot
Springs

385

385

Pactola
Reservoir

Hill
City

1880 Train

BLACK

NATIONAL

FOREST

Custer

JEWEL CAVE
NAT'L PARK

16

385

18

85

WYOMING

real thing! No samples are available at Homestake, but the museum and numerous other commercial attractions allow panning for gold. The value of what you find, if any, isn't even likely to cover the admission charge, but quite a few folks find it enjoyable.

Just four miles east of Lead is the colorful town of Deadwood. The town was built in a narrow gulch, so that it has only one important street – everything else is built precariously on the hillside. Although it definitely is a tourist trap these days (you'll encounter more souvenir and gift shops than anything else), it's still fun to walk around town and put your mind into an era long since vanished. **Mount Moriah Cemetery**, more commonly known as Boot Hill, contains the graves of a number of famous Western heroes and heroines, including Wild Bill Hickok and Calamity Jane. Other attractions include the **Ghosts of Deadwood Gulch-Western Heritage Museum**, a wax museum recounting the history of the area, and a tour of the **Broken Boot Gold Mine** (no longer active). Evening entertainment is varied, ranging from a reenactment of the **Trial of Jack McCall for the Murder of Wild Bill Hickok**, to legalized gambling.

From Deadwood backtrack towards Lead for two miles and go south on US 385 through the heart of the Black Hills National Forest. The scenery is lovely and quickly improves to beautiful in the vicinity of the **Pactola Reservoir**, about 25 miles south of Deadwood. There is a national forest visitor center at the reservoir which describes the management of the forest and offers information about recreation and sightseeing. Perhaps the most famous features of the Black Hills are in the southern portion of the region, but before getting on to them we're going to take a detour towards Rapid City (and then on to the Badlands).

Return north from the Pactola Reservoir for two miles to SR 44, which is locally known as Rim Rock Drive, and take a right. About 12 miles down the road are the **Black Hills Caverns**. Both 30-minute (easier and appropriate for senior citizens and those with minor disabilities) and 60-minute guided tours of the colorful cave are offered. You'll see stalactites, stalagmites and all those weird formations, complete with an explanation of how to distinguish one from the other. The Black Hills is an area famous for its caves and caverns. More than a half-dozen are operated commercially and there are also two run by the National Park Service: Jewel Cave and Wind Cave. We'll provide more details on Wind Cave when we reach that part of the route. The commercial variety are all of equal quality. We mentioned the Black Hills Caverns because they are conveniently on our route and are also the first you'll come upon. Others that you may wish to consider are **Beautiful Rushmore Cave** (Keystone), **Crystal Cave Park** (Rapid City), **Sitting Bull Crystal Caverns** (Rapid City), **Stagebarn Crystal Cave** (Piedmont) and **Wonderland Cave Natural Park** (Sturgis). **Jewel Cave National Park** is west of Custer.

Rapid City is one of South Dakota's largest communities, with over 55,000 people. It is the gateway to the Black Hills. The city has many art galleries and factories that produce Black Hills gold jewelry. The public is encouraged to visit and especially to *buy*.

Before entering town via SR 44, make a stop at the **Chapel in the Hills**. This striking structure is a copy of a famous Norwegian wooden stave church dating from the 12th century. Making it even more impressive is the fact that it's surrounded by hills on three sides – the front faces a broad valley, a setting not unlike those of Norway, except for the lack of a fjord.

Within the city are several interesting attractions. These include the **Museum of Geology**, on the campus of the School of Mines and Technology, and the **Dahl Fine Arts Center**. The highlight of the center is a 200-foot-long mural depicting America's first 200 years. A narration and special lighting accompany the mural.

From Rapid City we'll be heading eastbound on I-90. For those interested in the military, take Exit 66 to **Ellsworth Air Force Base**. Tours of the bomber and missile base are available by reservation. Call (605) 385-5189 for times and availability. The base is also the home of the **South Dakota Air and Space Museum**, which not only depicts the history of the base, but has a number of historic aircraft on display. Allow about 90 minutes for the combined tour and museum.

Now you're headed for the Badlands. A good place to make an overnight stay is in the town of Wall (Exit 110 on I-90). It's important that you stop in this town and pay a visit to the world famous **Wall Drug**. The place got started as a diner that advertised free water for travellers on US 14 in the days before the Interstate. Over the years, the place has grown by leaps and bounds and now covers several buildings running almost a full block and featuring everything from drugs and clothing to gift items and a restaurant. There are even several bands of mechanical figures to entertain visitors, one composed of bears, another featuring some shady looking rustlers! It's quite a fun place for adults and children and most of it is still free of charge, including that glass of water! Plan on spending as much as 45 minutes wandering around Wall Drug, excluding meal time and shopping.

Continue on I-90 eastbound to Exit 131 and turn right for the Cactus Flat entrance station of the incredible **Badlands National Park**. Badlands shows one of the world's finest examples of weathering and erosion over a time span of 80 million years. The name comes from the difficulty faced by those traveling the rocky and harsh terrain. Today, the route is easy and allows time to admire the beauty that coexists with the dark and forbidding landscape.

The Badlands Loop Road extends for 27 miles and covers most of the park (except for the very isolated southern unit). It rises, drops and winds this way and that, but is not at all difficult to negotiate. A total of 13 overlooks provide stunning vistas. All of these are clearly marked and you should stop at each one. Explanatory signs describe what you're looking at and its geologic history. The Cedar Pass Visitor Center is a good place to learn more about the Badlands. Some relatively short and easy Badland trails include the ¾-mile Door Trail leading to an opening in the rocks. Through the "door" is one of the very best views in the entire park. The Notch Trail is twice as long and somewhat more difficult; it requires visitors to scale a ladder. You can complete the loop road with all the overlooks and visitor center in under three hours. The above mentioned trails take about 90 minutes and two hours, respectively. Information on longer trails is available at the visitor center.

Upon leaving the park you'll reach I-90 in a couple of minutes. This time head west, back to Rapid City, using Exit 57 to gain access to I-190. This short road will take you into downtown. Turn left onto St. Joseph Street to 8th Street, which is US 16. Turn right and head south. Eighth Street becomes Mt. Rushmore Road as it leaves town. There are three points of interest on this road before you reenter the Black Hills National Forest. They're all located within a span of five miles, with the first attraction coming only three miles south of Rapid City. Stop number one is the **Marine Life Aquarium** which, in addition to display tanks of exotic fish, also has performing dolphins and seals, and a penguin exhibit. It may seem out of place in this part of the country, but it's a better than average aquarium and, for many people, a nice change of pace from the "Western" attractions you've seen so far. Allow at least 90 minutes. Just down the road are the **Black Hills Reptile**

Gardens. Don't be fooled by the name – this is an outstanding attraction, despite the fact that this (along with many other Black Hills sights) is "commercial." The Sky Dome reptile building houses truly unusual animals in a tropical setting. The multi-leveled facility is home to many types of snakes, birds, alligators and much more. There are also trained animal shows (no, the snakes don't perform). Another 90-minute minimum is required here. Finally, **Bear Country USA** is a drive-through safari park that focuses on large animals of North America. Again, 90 minutes is a suggested time frame for your visit to Bear Country.

Continue on US 16 until it reaches the junction of US 16A – head south three miles on this road to the town of Keystone. En route you'll pass through a tunnel. The Black Hills, especially the southern portion you're now entering, contain a lot of narrow roads with even narrower tunnels. While they're not overly difficult to drive a car on, trailers can be a problem. Some tunnels have bypasses for trailers (which can still be problematic for large vehicles), but others don't. If you're towing a trailer you should seek assistance from the auto club or South Dakota travel department to plan a suitable route.

Keystone is the nearest community to Mt. Rushmore. As such, many area attractions are related to the famous memorial created by Gutzon Borglum. The **Rushmore-Borglum Story** houses many of the artist's works along with much of his equipment. Allow about a half-hour (close to an hour if you plan to watch the 20-minute video on Mr. Borglum). The **Parade of Presidents Wax Museum** is adequately described by the title, although international figures of importance are also included. Allow another half-hour. Also in Keystone is the **Big Thunder Gold Mine**, a defunct 1880s mine. Guided tours lasting about 40 minutes are offered.

A mile south of Keystone turn right on SR 244. You'll immediately enter the **Mount Rushmore National Memorial**. We don't care how many times you've seen it in pictures or on film – nothing prepares you for this awe-inspiring sight. Viewing this should be mandatory for every American. If it doesn't bring a tear to your eye or a lump in your throat we suggest you have your emotions checked out by a professional. Many visitors are surprised to find that the memorial area is quite small. Leave your car in the very crowded parking lot and take a short trail leading from the excellent visitor center, with exhibits and film presentations on the sculptor, the process of creating the sculpture and the four presidents, down a paved promenade flanked by state flags. It ends at the viewing areas where you can stare at the 60-foot-high figures that have been chiseled into the top of the mountain.

While the heads of Washington, Jefferson, Lincoln and Teddy Roosevelt are both beautiful and inspiring during the day, the nighttime illumination brings new thrills. An outdoor amphitheater is the site of a talk given by a park ranger before the lights are turned on. Check at the visitor center for program time and bring a jacket as it's quite chilly in the evening. It's also a good idea to bring a cushion or something else to sit on as the stone benches, especially on cool nights, can freeze your rear! We might also add that the cafeteria, which looks out on the sculptures, is a good place to have dinner. Allow 90 minutes for your visit to Mt. Rushmore (excluding the illumination program).

Leaving Keystone, continue south on US 16. This stretch of the road is called the Norbeck Highway and is considered one of the great road building wonders of the world. The road rises in a series of sharp switchbacks called "spirals." Other roads in the vicinity use spirals to snake up, down, and through the mountains, but the Norbeck is the best of all. The views during the climb are fantastic, but are beaten when you finally reach the top of the spirals at the **Norbeck Overlook**. Here you can clearly see the distant sculptures of Mt. Rushmore. Binoculars bring them into sharp focus. On a sunny afternoon the view is nothing less than brilliant. After this dizzying ride, US 16A finally straightens out somewhat and enters the very large (73,000 acres) **Custer State Park**. Stay on US 16A until you reach the sign for the Wildlife Loop Road. This 18-mile loop is only partially paved, but not at all difficult to drive. It's well maintained and travels through grasslands and rolling hills. You'll see plenty of wildlife along the way, including a 1,400-strong bison herd, elk, bighorn sheep and many others. Stay in your car with the windows closed as these animals are in *their* natural habitat and are wild. The loop returns you to US 16A. Go one mile east and turn left on SR 87, known as the Needles Highway. This is the most spectacular portion of the park and offers the best scenery. The extremely narrow 14-mile road twists its way through an endless series of colorful and oddly shaped rock pinnacles and spires. There are sharp turns and several more tunnels that can only take one car at a time; sound your horn as you approach each one and proceed when it's clear. The highlight of the Needles Highway is a formation known as The Eye of the Needle. No name could be more appropriate for this tall, thin rock spire, complete with an opening at the top. There are several places, including at "The Eye," to pull off the road and take a better look at the scenery. The Needles section also is the home of previously mentioned Mt. Haney and majestic Sylvan Lake, both flanked by the wonderful formations. A minimum of 2½ hours is needed to go through these two sections of Custer State Park (that is, the Wildlife Loop Road and the Needles). This does not include an ascent of the Sunday Gulch Foot Trail which drops 800 feet towards the lake. The trail is mainly paved, but has many steps and is not an easy climb if you're out of shape.

SR 87 ends at the junction of US 16 and 385. For another view of the Black Hills, head north for three miles to Hill City, home of **1880 Train**. Two-hour narrated rides through the hills to Keystone are given several times each day. It's a relaxing way to see the Black Hills although you don't see much more than is covered on this driving tour. The train ride can also be taken from Keystone.

In any event, either from the end of the Needles Highway or from Hill City, head south on US 385 (also west US 16) to the town of Custer. Five miles north of town is the **Crazy Horse Memorial**. The sculpture, in the best traditions of Mt. Rushmore, honors the famous Indian chief. When completed by the descendants of Gutzon Borglum (no scheduled date – it's slow going), the massive carving of the Indian chief on his white horse will be the largest statue in the world, measuring 563 feet in height and 641 feet across. The center includes models of the statue, an explanation of the ongoing work and a fine museum on the Indians of North America that should not be missed. If you're lucky, you might see some blasting. Allow at least an hour.

Another interesting attraction here is the **National Museum of Woodcarving**. The figures are mostly animated and occupy handcarved furnishings. Most depict humorous characters or situations. Allow at least a half-hour. Custer is also a popular place for taking balloon rides over the Black Hills. For children there is **Flintstones Bedrock City** about which no more need be said.

Approximately 21 miles south of Custer via US 385 is the entrance to **Wind Cave National Park**. This is one of the largest and most attractive caves in the Black Hills. There are five different guided tours lasting between one and four hours. Generally speaking, the longer trips are the most difficult, with the four-hour adventure being only for spelunkers.

Eight miles south of the cave is Hot Springs town and another mile southwest from there on the US 18 Bypass is an outstanding attraction simply called the **Mammoth Site**. A large number of bones from Columbian era mammoths were found at a spot believed to have been a natural spring-fed depression. The remains are approximately 26,000 years old, far younger than dinosaur remains and in much better shape. What makes the Mammoth Site unusual is that there hasn't been any depletion of the bones by archaeological researchers or others. There are guided tours as well as a paleontology museum. Allow at least an hour.

From Hot Springs head west on US 18, which will cross back into Wyoming after 12 miles. At Mule Creek Junction it joins US 85 and heads south. Unfortunately the next 100 miles is not a particularly interesting stretch of highway, but at least the road is easy to drive on. You can break up the ride at the approximate half-way point in Lusk by paying a brief visit to the **Stagecoach Museum** on Main Street. Accommodations can also be found here. At the town of Lingle head west on US 26 to Fort Laramie and then three miles southwest following signs to **Fort Laramie National Historic Site**. The fort was an important point on the Oregon Trail until 1890. Many buildings have been restored and refurnished to appear as they did during the period of the fort's greatest activity. There is a museum telling the fort's history and costumed staff demonstrate life and activities at the post as they were in the 1870s. Allow about an hour for your visit.

Other interesting aspects of life on the Oregon Trail are in evidence a bit further west on US 26 in Guernsey. The **Oregon Trail Ruts State Historic Site** (one mile south of town) and **Register Cliff State Historic Site** (three miles south) are two such places. The former depicts 19th-century pioneer life and trails take you past actual ruts remaining from the days of the wagon trains. The latter is a 100-foot-high cliff where many westward bound settlers inscribed their names. Local history is also on display at the **Guernsey State Park Museum**, northwest of town via SR 317. From Guernsey continue west on US 26 to the junction of I-25. Take I-25 south back to Cheyenne, the starting and finishing point of our journey through beautiful Wyoming.

Alternative Routes

No state as large as Wyoming can be covered in a single loop trip. While we attempted to cover the highlights within the time and mileage constraints we discussed, there are things that had to be bypassed. For those of you who want to see more, these alternative routes are the answer. After taking you through two alternatives, we'll describe a few short excursions that can be done on the main route, as well as one that complements an alternative route.

The Southern Frontier

This alternative routing departs from the main suggested route immediately upon leaving Cheyenne and doesn't rejoin it until Jackson and Grand Teton National Park. It is about 120 miles longer than the base route.

Head west on US 80 from Cheyenne to Laramie, a distance of 50 miles. Before town, stop at a rest area on I-80 at Sherman; there's a 42-foot-high statue – the **Abraham Lincoln Memorial Monument**.

Laramie is the third largest city in the state and home to the **University of Wyoming**. The campus covers almost 800 acres just north of downtown and features three museums with such diverse fields as Anthropology, Art and Geology. The **Kennedy/Watt American Heritage Center** has a varied display of documents and Americana. You'll find, for example, Jack Benny's violin and Hopalong Cassidy's six-guns! Allow a minimum of two hours to tour all of the museums and the Heritage Center. The **Laramie Plains Museum** is housed in the restored Victorian home of one of the town's earliest residents. It depicts local history and contains period furnishings.

Two longer attractions, both worthwhile if you have the time, are the **Wyoming Territorial Park** and the **Wyoming/Colorado Scenic Railroad**. The park recreates a Wyoming town from the 1870s. Visitors can watch and participate in craft activities and daily routines of the period, witness a prison escape and help recapture the felons, visit a restored territorial prison and view the archaeological work being done on the site. There is also a short train ride. A visit to the Territorial Park requires at least three hours. Twice that amount of time is needed to take the railroad, which heads south and crosses the border into Colorado. The ride covers high plains and mountains of the Snowy Range. The scenery is beautiful, maybe not as spectacular as on the Silverton in Durango, Colorado, but still well worth seeing. Reservations are required. A wide variety of lodging and dining establishments can be found in Laramie, almost all adjacent to the Interstate.

Less than two hours west of Laramie via I-80 is Rawlins, once a notorious frontier town and now an important agricultural community. Of interest in town is the local history **Carbon County Museum** and the more fascinating **Wyoming Frontier Prison**, which operated for 80 years before closing in 1981. Hour-long tours visit the cell blocks and death row. This may be too gruesome for some younger children (and squeamish adults). West of Rawlins on I-80 you'll pass a large sandstone rock formation known as **Table Rock**. Along the 30-mile stretch that includes Table Rock, the road parallels the Continental Divide, crossing it at one point. The scenery is excellent. Still further west at Exit 104 is the town of Rock Springs. It has a population of almost 20,000 people and is a good place to stay overnight. The town is the gateway point for interesting side trips into the large sand dune region north of town and the scenery of Flaming Gorge National Recreation Area to the south. The trip to Flaming Gorge adds a loop of another 150 miles and is described later as a side trip.

Continue west on I-80 until just past the town of Little America (accommodations available) at Exit 66 and take US 30 west for 46 miles to Kemmerer, another option for overnight stays. This town's claim to fame is the fact that J.C. Penny opened his very first store here in 1902. His former home is in town. Eleven miles west, still on US 30, is **Fossil Butte National Monument**. The colorful butte is almost 1,000 feet high and contains the fossil remains of freshwater fish that lived approximately 50 million years ago. Fossils can be viewed along one of two trails and at the visitor center. The trails include some steep climbs and require a minimum of two hours.

Continue on US 30 for 44 miles before skirting the Idaho border by taking SR 89 for 13 miles to Geneva and US 89. Head north on US 89. The scenery will immediately change from pleasant to beautiful as the road travels along the southern edge of the Bridger-Teton National Forest. An interesting stop can be made in Afton, which was originally a Mormon settlement. You can learn about the town by visiting the **Lincoln County Daughters of Utah Pioneer Museum** (don't worry – you aren't lost – you're still in Wyoming). A real sight is the large arch that spans the main street. It's composed of more than 3,000 elk antlers! **Periodic Spring** is a nearby attraction that's unusual in that it's a cold-water geyser, a geological rarity. It's located in the national forest five miles east of town. Accommodations and food can be found in Afton and, 26 miles further along US 89, in Alpine. After Alpine take US 26/89 as it heads through the breathtakingly beautiful Grand Canyon of the Snake River in the Bridger-Teton National Forest. You'll see people rafting the Snake River 100 feet or more below the ledge on which you're riding. The entire 35-mile stretch from Alpine to Jackson, where we rejoin the main itinerary, is one of the most scenic roads to be found in Wyoming.

The Shell Canyon Route

This short alternative goes from Cody to Burgess Junction via US 14/16/20 (instead of US 14A that we took on the main route). This trip is actually a few miles less than the base route.

The only major town on this path is Greybull. Two interesting museums are located here. The first is the **Greybull Museum** which focuses mainly on natural history. The **Greybull Wildlife Museum** features mounted animal specimens in recreated natural settings. You can visit both museums in under an hour.

Known as the Big Horn Scenic Byway, US 14 takes you over the Bighorn Mountains and the Granite Pass at an elevation of 8,950 feet. The highlight of the route is the **Shell Canyon and Falls**, where an overlook provides a wonderful view of the sheer cliffs that flank the deep, narrow gorge. There are several trails for those who wish to explore the gorge in greater detail or want to get closer to the falls.

Other Side Trips

The Wind River Canyon

This is a 70-mile round trip departing from and returning to the main route at the town of Shoshoni. Immediately upon leaving

Shoshoni the road is edged by the **Boysen Reservoir**. The deep blue waters are surrounded on three sides by a rocky high desert plateau. However, one side is impounded by red sandstone cliffs rising almost perpendicular to the lake and providing a beautiful contrast to the color of the water. The **Wind River Canyon** stretches for 32 miles from Shoshoni to just south of Thermopolis. The highway is an engineering marvel, having been blasted through solid rock in many places. There are three tunnels where the engineers couldn't otherwise get the road around the rocks. The canyon, besides having towering cliffs, is dotted with unusual rock formations, the most prominent being Chimney Rock, 10 miles south of Thermopolis. Formations are identified by signs located in frequent pull outs. Due to the high altitude along the Wind River Canyon, the loftiest mountain peaks are covered by snow and ice even during the middle of the summer.

The town of Thermopolis is best known for the **Hot Springs State Park**. Within the park are numerous mineral baths, springs and thermal terraces. The Bighorn Hot Springs, with a daily output of around 2.8 million gallons of water, is one of the world's largest. An unusual feature of the park is the hot waterfalls. All the pools and baths are open to the public free of charge – a legacy that dates back to an agreement made with the Indians that everyone would have access to the baths. It's probably one of the few Indian treaties that we haven't broken.

This side trip can be completed in about three hours, excluding time added for lunch and taking to the waters at Hot Springs Park.

The Lower Wind River Basin

Originating in Riverton, just 22 miles past Shoshoni once you've returned to the main route from the Wind River Canyon, this 120-mile excursion returns to the suggested main trip 36 miles northwest of Riverton.

Passing through the town of Lander, proceed for nine miles southwest on SR 131 to the **Sinks Canyon State Park**. Here you'll find a series of lovely waterfalls connected by a 1½-mile easy trail that goes through a gorge complete with whitewater rapids. The park also has a visitor center to explain the natural and human history of the area. Return to Lander via SR 131 and then US 287 south for nine miles where you'll pick up SR 28 south. Off of this road, following signs, is the town of **South Pass City**. The small community was once a successful mining town. About 25 buildings remain from the 1860s and have been partially restored. Restoration work continues. After South Pass City reverse your route to Lander, but this time continue north on US 287 back to the main route at the junction of US 26. The entire side excursion can be completed in about four hours.

Ten Sleep Canyon

This is a 130-mile round trip from Buffalo and returning to the same spot. The route follows US 16, called the Cloud Peak Skyway. The road is a magnificent mountain highway, crossing the Powder River Pass at an elevation of 9,686 feet. You'll travel on US 16 as far as the western edge of the Bighorn National Forest (63 miles from Buffalo). This allows you to see the most beautiful section of **Ten Sleep Canyon**. The canyon area contains a fish hatchery and fish rearing station where visitors are welcome. As this side trip is essentially a drive and view excursion, it can be completed in under three hours.

Flaming Gorge

This trip is located on the "Southern Frontier" alternative route, departing from Rock Springs and following a U-shaped course for approximately 150 miles before returning to I-80 at the town of Green River, a few miles west of Rock Springs.

The sole star of this trip is the **Flaming Gorge National Recreation Area**, the majority of which is situated in Wyoming, with some parts extending into the northern portion of Utah. Take US 191 south from Rock Springs. The road heads through mountainous terrain for 51 miles to the Utah line and another 11 miles to Dutch John, where your tour of Flaming Gorge begins. Here is the Flaming Gorge Dam and Visitor Center. There are tours of the dam (both guided and self guided) which is 500 feet high and 1,300 feet across the top. The best views are from the top of the dam itself. All kinds of water sports are available in Dutch John as are overnight accommodations.

Proceed south on US 191 from Dutch John for eight miles to the junction of UT 44. Along this route are many highlights. The Red Canyon Visitor Center has exhibits and you can look down the sheer drop of 1,400 feet to the vivid blue lake from a series of viewpoints that are connected by an easy nature trail. The Jones

Hole National Fish Hatchery is two miles past the visitor center. There is a trail here that enters a narrow and beautiful canyon surrounded by towering walls nearly 2,000 feet high.

Continuing on UT 44 will bring you to Manila where you pick up SR 530 and cross the border into Wyoming. You can also take the Sheep Creek Loop, a 13-mile road that also returns you to UT 44 and Manila. The road is a bit difficult, but is picturesque and has access to trails with a significant amount of fossils. Once you get to SR 530 the road travels along the western edge of the recreation area. The scenery is pleasant and there are various recreational water activities on the way. The Flaming Gorge loop will require nearly a full day to complete. Extra time should be allowed for those who wish to go boating, fishing or swimming.

Chapter 2

Montana

The Big Sky Country

Montana is the fourth largest state in the United States, so naturally it takes a big sky to cover it. As is the case in most large western states, topographic diversity is to be expected. And you certainly get it here. The western third of Montana is the northern Rockies at its most awesome, while the remainder of the state is dominated by the Great Plains. There is little transition – the Rockies start quite abruptly at the edge of the Great Plains and rise sharply. It is also a state that is rich in Western history. Cowboys and Indians come alive in its museums, old towns and famous battlefield sites. The outdoor way of life dominates in Montana. Even its cities, none of which has more than 85,000 people, are just minutes away from beautiful wilderness areas. This is where you can get away from it all. The entire state population of approximately 800,000 is spread over 147,000 square miles, making it the least densely-populated state in the nation, except for Alaska. An excellent road system allows visitors to see Montana's many natural and man-made wonders. So, without further ado, we give you the Big Sky Country!

Along the Suggested Itinerary

While our trip originates in Billings, any number of the state's cities could be substituted if they have better flight or road connections from your home. These include Bozeman, Helena, Missoula and Great Falls. Vacationers arriving by car will be using one of four major roads – I-15 from the south (join at Butte), I-90 from the southeast (Billings), I-94 from the east (Billings) or I-90 from the west (Missoula).

Nothing could be simpler than arriving in Billings (or the other gateway cities) by air. The small airport is only two miles from downtown and with the lack of both air and ground traffic you should be touring within a half-hour of landing! The first attraction, in fact, is located immediately opposite the airport entrance. The **Peter Yegen Jr. Yellowstone County Museum** features displays and artifacts that chronicle the routine of everyday life on the frontier. Another museum, this one geared more towards local and area history, is the **Western Heritage Center** in the center of downtown. The collection is set in a 1901 structure that originally served as a library. On Division Street, also downtown, is the **Moss Mansion**. Built in 1903, the building is furnished in period and remains almost exactly as it was during its hey-day. It provides a very realistic glimpse into the life of a wealthy family during turn-of-the-century Montana.

The city of Billings, with over 80,000 residents (the most populous in the state), is backed by the 400-foot-high cliffs of the Rim Rocks along the Yellowstone River. A scenic drive called the **Chief Black Otter Trail** traverses the Rim Rocks for about four miles in the northeastern corner of the city. An outstanding view of Billings is available from almost anywhere along this drive, but nowhere is it better than at the large bronze statue of a cowboy and his horse titled the **Range Rider of the Yellowstone**. The statue is on the Chief Black Otter Trail and you should allow about 45 minutes to drive the trail and stop at the statue.

Five miles west of downtown via Exit 446 of I-90 is **Oscar's Dreamland**. This is the largest collection of farm equipment in the country. There are also a number of pioneer buildings that have been brought to this site from various places around the state, covered wagons and rides on a miniature railroad. Allow between one and two hours for your stay at Oscar's.

Billings, with its convenient Interstate location, has a wide choice of lodging facilities and restaurants. For evening entertainment, the most popular diversion in summer is the **Billings Night Rodeo**. A barbecue precedes the rodeo and the entire event is an enjoyable night out.

Upon leaving Billings plan for a long stretch of Interstate driving; it's about 120 miles west to the town of Livingston. The drive is a breeze, however, and can be easily accomplished in two hours. For those who must stop (or have kids that are constantly asking "are we there yet?"), the **Big Timber Waterslide** in Big Timber is a water-based amusement park between Billings and Livingston that can cool things off.

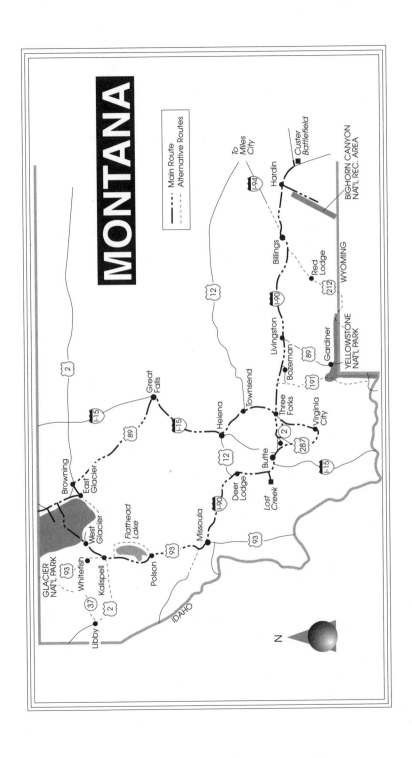

MONTANA

Main Route
Alternative Routes

GLACIER NAT'L PARK

Libby

37

Kalispell
2

Whitefish
93

West Glacier

Flathead Lake

East Glacier

Browning

89

Polson

93

Missoula

93

Deer Lodge

I-90

Lost Creek

Butte

12

I-15

287

2

Virginia City

Three Forks

Helena

Townsend

12

I-15

Great Falls

I-15

2

To Miles City

I-94

Hardin

Custer Battlefield

Billings

I-90

Livingston

Bozeman

89

191

Gardiner

Red Lodge

212

YELLOWSTONE NAT'L PARK

WYOMING

BIGHORN CANYON NAT'L REC. AREA

IDAHO

N

Livingston is located at the beginning of the Paradise Valley, a scenic area at the foothills of the sharply rising Rockies that serves as a gateway to Yellowstone National Park (see the Alternative Routes section for ways of combining Yellowstone with a Montana loop). The Yellowstone River runs through town and several ranges of the Rockies form a majestic backdrop to the west. Livingston, which has several nice lodging establishments, is a small town, but doesn't lack for museums. The **Depot Center Museum** and the **Park County Museum** both chronicle area history, especially the importance of the Northern Pacific Railroad. The Depot Center is in a former train station built in extravagant Italian Renaissance style and concentrates solely on the railroad. The Park County Museum also pays attention to other aspects of the frontier settlement. Each should take about a half-hour. Finally, the **Lone Wolf Wildlife Museum** features numerous realistic dioramas of big game animals.

Another 23 miles west of Livingston on I-90 is Bozeman. A fair size town by Montana standards, Bozeman is also a place where you won't have any trouble finding a bed for the night. Here, too, are several museums. The best is the large **Museum of the Rockies**, located opposite the football stadium on Montana State University, south of downtown. The museum is housed in an attractive modern structure and the natural history of the Rockies is explored through dioramas and exhibits, including full-size dinosaur replicas. Allow at least 45 minutes for this museum. Other interesting museums with Montana or Western themes are the **Gallatin County Pioneer Museum** on West Main Street and the **American Computer Museum**. The latter seems totally unrelated to anything in Bozeman (we can't figure out how it wound up here), but is still interesting. It traces the development of these regulators of modern day life from their early origins to the present.

After leaving Bozeman continue west on I-90 for 30 more miles to the Three Forks exit. The first place of interest in the vicinity is six miles northeast of town following signs for Trident. This is the **Missouri Headwaters State Park**. It was here in 1805 that the Lewis and Clark expedition discovered the headwaters of the Missouri River, which is formed by the joining of the Madison, Gallatin and Jefferson Rivers. The park contains an overlook where you can look down upon the wide gorge and see where the rivers merge.

Seven miles south of Three Forks is the **Madison Buffalo Jump State Historic Site**. Here, you will learn how the Indians hunted buffalo by stampeding them over the cliffs. There are several such sites in Montana, but this is one of the better ones. A visitor center fully explains in words, drawings and dioramas this 2,000-year-old hunting technique. Allow about a half-hour.

Return to I-90 westbound, but only for one exit. From there take SR 2 heading west. About 15 miles from Three Forks is the **Lewis and Clark Caverns State Park**. The large park contains lovely mountain scenery as well as a beautiful limestone cavern known for its large rooms, complicated passageways and colorful formations. Guided tours last two hours and include a rather strenuous climb up the hillside to the cave entrance. Although this is a first-rate attraction, you have to be in reasonably good health to enjoy it. The trek up to the entrance requires a bit of stamina.

Upon completion of the caverns, retrace your route on SR 2 for a couple of miles to the junction of US 287 and head south. By this time you're really into the Rockies. The 35 miles on US 287 are quite scenic as you ride through the Madison Valley, flanked by the Madison and Tobacco Root Mountain ranges and the Beaverhead National Forest.

At the town of Ennis leave US 287 for SR 287 (who dreamed up this numbering system? – it's terribly confusing!) for 14 miles to **Virginia City**. This was once a successful mining community and was given renewed fame this century by the *Bonanza* television program, which is set here. During the "good old days" as many as 190 murders were committed here by a notorious gang over a six month period. The miners formed a group called the Vigilantes who brought their own style of justice to Virginia City, hanging 21 of the outlaws. Today, Virginia City has only 100 residents, but the town is humming as a living museum. About two dozen of the buildings from the mid-1860s have been painstakingly restored to give visitors a glimpse into the past. Nevada City is just two miles west of Virginia City and is similar, but not as large or as well developed.

While in Virginia City be sure to visit the **Spencer Watkins Memorial Museum** of pioneer history and some of the restored buildings, especially the ornate **Virginia City Opera House**. Entertainment in the form of late 19th-century music hall programs is offered at the Opera House as well as at the **Gilbert Brewery**.

Another diversion in town is the **Alder Gulch Work Train**. This makes a one-hour excursion between Virginia and Nevada Cities.

You should allow a half-day for touring the Virginia City area. There are overnight accommodations here, but they're limited in number and quality of rooms. You may find it better to stay in Ennis or about 20 miles past Virginia City on SR 287 in Sheridan.

From Virginia City proceed on SR 287 to the town of Twin Bridges where you'll pick up SR 41 northbound. This soon runs back into SR 2. Head west, entering the Deerlodge National Forest and crossing the Continental Divide at the Pipestone Pass (elevation 6,418 feet). SR 2 carries you straight into Butte.

As is the case with most of the larger communities in Montana, Butte began in the heady days of gold fever. Although large quantities of gold and silver were never found in Butte, it did become one of the largest and most successful mining sites for copper. The name of the "richest hill on earth" was given to Butte in recognition of the vast seams of copper found here. Mining the ore was essentially abandoned in the mid-1950s after it became too expensive to extract from the ground. The open pit Berkeley Mine is a testament to the glory days of the past and the town offers many attractions related to the story of copper mining.

The **Copper King Mansion** (W. Granite Street) was built in 1884 by the richest of the many copper barons who made their fortunes in Montana. Guided tours of the plush 32-room Victorian mansion last about 40 minutes. The **Mineral Museum** (Park Street on the campus of the Montana Technical College) takes a scientific look at the natural riches of Montana. Also on display is the largest gold nugget ever found in the state. The most entertaining look at Butte's mining past is found on Park Street near downtown in the **World Museum of Mining and Hell-Roarin' Gulch**. The indoor portion of the museum displays mining equipment and exhibits on mining techniques and depicts the colorful story of Butte's pioneer days. The outdoor section, located on the site of an old mine, is a recreation of a mining camp and Western town. Allow at least an hour for the World Museum.

Another way to take in the sights is to ride on **Old Number 1**, a replica streetcar that carries visitors through town on a 90-minute guided tour. The tour doesn't inlcude time at any of the museums, so take this ride only if you have time to spare.

One of the Butte area's most unusual features can't be reached by car as it's located on a private road. **Our Lady of the Rockies** is a gigantic (90-foot-high) statue of the Virgin Mary. Despite the nature of the statue, Our Lady of the Rockies is considered to be a non-denominational tribute to motherhood. Two round trips by bus are available each day and last two hours. They depart from 434 N. Main Street (unless the weather is bad). The statue is perched directly on the Continental Divide and the trip offers spectacular views. The lady took six years to build and required the use of the Air National Guard to bring the pieces of the statue up into the mountains.

Butte has many choices for overnights stays, mostly along the Interstate and representing a number of the major chains. You'll use I-90 westbound to leave town, traveling towards Deer Lodge. Why this is two words when the Deerlodge Forest is only one is beyond us – we can't seem to find an explanation. In any event, as the route between these two locations runs along the National Forest there is ample mountain scenery to keep you amused. You'll be taking a little detour, however, before getting there. Leave the Interstate at Exit 208 and head west to the town of Anaconda via SR 1, then north on County Route 273, following signs to the **Lost Creek State Park**. In this lovely park, covered with evergreens and aspens, is a deep canyon. A small river plunges over a series of rocks and disappears into the dark canyon. After visiting the park head back on Route 273, this time heading north towards Galen until you reach I-90 once again. Allow about 90 minutes for Lost Creek, which includes the time to and from I-90.

Back on I-90 it's a short ride to the exit (#187) for Deer Lodge. While Butte is still dominated by its mining past, Deer Lodge's attractions are of a different nature, even though it, too, owes its origins to mining. Three attractions are conveniently located just blocks off the Interstate, adjacent to one another on lower Main Street. These are the **Old Montana Prison, Towe Ford Museum**, and **Yesterday's Playthings Doll & Toy Museum**. The prison has the option of either self-guided or guided tours in summer (about 90 minutes for the guided tour; less if you go alone). Your visit includes a walk through cell blocks, maximum security center, and the walled prison compound. The prison is home of the Montana Law Enforcement Museum. This has a collection of weapons and uniforms and a memorial to Montana policemen and women killed in the line of duty.

The Ford Museum is one of the most comprehensive collections of automobiles produced by the Ford Motor Company in the entire world. More than 100 vehicles are on display, from the earliest 1903 models through the 1960s. Allow about 45 minutes to cruise the museum. The final member of this interesting trio of attractions is a huge collection of dolls from all over the globe. Although other types of toys are also featured, it's the dolls that are the stars of the show. It requires at least a half-hour to see everything in Yesterday's Playthings.

Head north on Main Street and at the northern edge of town you'll reach the final Deer Lodge attraction, the **Grant-Kohrs Ranch National Historic Site**. The 1,500-acre ranch is only the remnant of a much larger ranch that was established in the 1860s. The focal point of the site today is the 23-room ranch house, where rangers give guided tours. Visitors may explore the grounds on their own, passing by some of the 80-odd buildings that remain from the original ranch. Details on self-guided tours are available at the information center. Allow about 90 minutes for a complete visit to Grant-Kohrs.

Deer Lodge has several nice motels if you need to spend the night here. Leaving Deer Lodge we'll head west once again on I-90 for the 75-mile trip to Missoula, home of the University of Montana and one of the state's largest cities, with a population of 43,000. As usual, we'll address the in-town attractions first.

The **Historical Museum at Fort Missoula** (Exit 105, follow US 12 to South Avenue) is on the site where Missoula began as an outpost during the conflict with the Nez Perce Indians. At press time only half of the fort's original structures had been restored, but more might be completed by the time you visit. Allow a minimum of a half-hour to take a self-guided tour of the fort. Downtown on W. Pine Street is the **St. Francis Xavier Church**, whose steeple rises to a height of 144 feet and is much admired for its fine stained glass windows. West on Business Route I-90 is the **Rocky Mountain Elk Foundation & Wildlife Visitor Center.** This is another collection of stuffed animals, concentrating on elk, but also featuring other big game. Many of the specimens on display here are of record-breaking size. It won't take more than a half-hour to visit unless you opt to watch the wildlife films.

Two attractions are located west of the city. The first is the **Smokejumpers Base Aerial Fire Depot** adjacent to Missoula's airport on W. Broadway. An exhibit area has displays on the fire fighters of the Forest Service. In addition, actual "smokejumpers" give tours of the facility and explain some of the techniques used in combating forest fires. Allow about an hour for the combined tour and exhibit area.

Twelve miles northwest of town is the **Snowbowl Ski Area**. Although primarily a winter sports area, the summer season makes use of the chairlifts to carry visitors to the 7,600-foot summit. From the top you'll have a panoramic view of the Bitteroot Mountains as well as being able to peer down on Missoula. Allow an hour for the round trip, including time at the top.

Missoula has dozens of motels and hotels, including the big chains. Restaurants also abound. 4B's Family Restaurant chain is a good choice. They can be found in larger towns throughout Montana and have good family fare at very reasonable prices.

We leave the Interstate eight miles west of Missoula and head north on US 93, passing through the Flathead Indian Reservation. The first stop is the **National Bison Range** off US 93 near the town of Ravalli (27 miles north of I-90) via SRs 200 and 212. More than 400 buffalo make the range their home. Visitors will see various breeds of sheep as well as deer and elk. There are two auto tours (both on unpaved roads). The short tour can be done in about a half-hour, while the longer one covers 19 miles and requires almost two hours. In either case, you must stay in your vehicle at all times. Trailers are forbidden on the longer route, which has some very steep grades. Pull over to the side when viewing the animals so that others may pass. Before venturing out on either auto tour stop at the visitor center and take in its informative displays.

Back on US 93 it's only a few miles to the **St. Ignatius Mission**, established by Jesuits in 1854. There is a small museum about Indians and religious artifacts, but the highlight here is the church. It contains almost 60 frescos painted at the turn of the century by the mission's cook. A bit further north bird lovers can stop at the **Ninepipe National Wildlife Refuge** to admire several breeds of waterfowl.

Another short ride brings you to the town of Polson, located at the southern edge of beautiful Flathead Lake, a gem in the mountains. If you're here during May or June you'll gasp in awe as a half-million gallons of water per second rushes through the 500-foot-high walls of the **Flathead River Gorge.** At other times the flow is greatly reduced, although the gorge itself is still a pretty sight. **Flathead Lake** is the largest natural fresh-water lake in the United States west of the Mississippi River. Fishing and boating are popular in many state parks along the lake's eastern and western shores. Our route goes up the west shore along US 93. You can take a boat ride on the *Port Polson Princess*. There are two rides offered: the first takes 90 minutes, the second three hours.

Also in town are two small museums, the pioneer-themed **Polson-Flathead Historical Museum** and the **Miracle of America Museum**. The latter is a mixed bag of items ranging from pioneer artifacts to military weapons to the Hall of Fame of Montana Fiddlers! One can only wonder how that got mixed in with the others. Polson has most of the motels and resorts in the Flathead Lake area, although accommodations can also be found in Lakeside, a half-hour north of Polson on the western shore. US 93 hugs the west side of the lake while SRs 35 and 2 go up the east side where they rejoin US 93. The east side is more scenic, providing better mountain views along a less developed shoreline, but US 93 is easier to drive. The mileage isn't significantly different from one to the other.

The town of Kalispell lies 53 miles north of Polson along US 93. Located in a scenic valley, the town is the center of Montana's cherry growing area. There are boat rides on Flathead Lake available here, the 90-minute trip on the *Far West Cruise Ship* being one of the most popular. Kalispell is the location of the **Conrad Mansion National Historic Site**. The Victorian edifice contains 26 rooms and was built by the town's founder in 1895. Self-guided tours require a half-hour and pass through the elegantly furnished rooms. A side trip departs from Kalispell and is described later in this chapter.

From Kalispell head east on US 2 for 20 minutes to Columbia Falls. The town contains the **Big Sky Waterslide** amusement park where you can satisfy the children's need to play at their games. A road leading four miles east brings you to the **Hungry Horse Dam**. Guided tours are offered, but the short ride off the main route is worth it just for the great view of the Hungry Horse Reservoir surrounded by lofty mountains.

Soon after returning to an easterly course on US 2 you'll come upon the **Glacier Maze**. Patterned after similar "parks" on the grounds of some of Europe's most famous palaces, the maze is a confusing grouping of high hedges with intricate passageways where you attempt to find your way through to the end. This one has two routes, one being easier than the other. All in all, they cover more than a mile and can be a real challenge. Don't worry, if you're really lost there are "emergency" exits. But, in all seriousness, if you are claustrophobic the maze may not be the best place for you to visit. For most people about an hour is sufficient time to chart your way through the maze.

The scenery gets better with every mile you travel in this area because you're approaching one of the scenic highlights of America – **Glacier National Park**. The entrance is just 15 miles east of Columbia Falls on US 2 at the town of West Glacier. The town has plenty of accommodation options and there are several hotels within the park itself. See the Addendum for details. West Glacier is the departure point for most scenic rafting and whitewater trips on the Flathead River. These range in length from a half-day to almost a week. Telephone numbers of some operators are given in the Addendum.

Your visit to Glacier National Park will be a memorable one as it contains what is perhaps the finest mountain scenery in the United States. The mountains are covered by more than 50 glaciers and contain some 200 lakes. The green meadows are colored with wild flowers during the summer.

The most famous part of the park, but certainly not all there is to see within its 1,600 square miles, lies on the 51-mile "Going to the Sun Road," which connects the West entrance at West Glacier with the Eastern entrance at the town of St. Mary. Not only does this road offer some of the most brilliant of Glacier's sights, but it is, in itself, an engineering feat to be admired. Despite the high rocky mountains, sharp turns and grades (including a pass through the Continental Divide at 6,680 feet), the ride is one that can be undertaken by all but the novice driver. Just go slow around those turns and along the edge of precipitous ledges. That way you'll safely enjoy the journey and the scenery.

The road has 17 overlooks, each one being worth a stop. After riding beside 10-mile-long Lake MacDonald, the park's largest lake, you'll emerge from the forest and see the panoramic backdrop of high mountains. The road begins to climb quickly and dramatically towards the Continental Divide. Take some time out for the short Trail of the Cedars to view magnificent trees and a rushing river. Longer hikes also begin here that lead into a beautiful gorge. Returning to your car now, the road clings to the mountain ledge that drops off to the rocky terrain below. It winds its way around the peaks with water cascading down the sheer mountain walls and onto the roadway from melting glaciers. In some areas the ice almost touches the road, especially during early summer. The scenery surrounds you as the switchbacks carry you up and down and around to the Logan Pass Visitor Center. The main information center within the park, it is also the starting point for many walks in the high alpine meadows. A section of the Continental Divide known as the Hanging Gardens can be seen from a fairly long but easy trail. Even if you don't get into exploring the trails of the Logan Pass area, do take some time to just sit down in the meadow and relax.

After Logan Pass the road starts to descend quickly before traveling along St. Mary's Lake. Sun Point has a beautiful vista and there's a short trail to the Baring Falls. Soon after Sun Point you'll reach the St. Mary's entrance. However, you're not done with Glacier National Park yet. From St. Mary's head north via US 89 for nine miles to the town of Babb. Go east along a good, paved 13-mile road into Glacier Park's outstanding Many Glacier Region. At the end of this road, which has wonderful views of lakes and mountains, you'll reach Swiftcurrent Lake, a lovely mountain-ringed glacial lake. The stately wooden lodge here is the starting point for many trails leading along and around the lake and, for the more adventurous, into the interior.

Upon finishing your visit to Many Glacier, return to Babb. Although you can continue along the main route on our Montana journey, we include here, rather than as a side trip, a short excursion north of the Canadian border to **Waterton Lakes National Park**. The park is reached by traveling 32 miles north from Babb on the highly scenic Chief Mountain International Highway. Waterton Lakes is physically attached to the top of Glacier National Park. Boat rides on Waterton Lake offer breathtaking mountain vistas and actually travel across the border back into the United States where you can get out and stretch your legs on an easy and short wilderness trail. No roads lead into this portion of the park – the only other way to get here besides the boat trip is by a multi-day hike from other sections on the American side. Wildlife along the shoreline is plentiful and frequently seen by visitors from the boat. Waterton Lakes also features a quaint town in the middle of the park where deer and other animals freely roam the streets. Attractive Cameron Falls and the colorful Red Rock Canyon are other attractions within the park that are worth a visit.

Return to Babb from Waterton by reversing your route but, when you reach Babb, continue south on US 89 to Kiowa and then take SR 49 along Glacier National Park's eastern edge. There's a side road (unpaved) leading into the Belly River Country of Glacier. The area is beautiful, but is mainly popular with backpackers as there are few facilities and no easy or short trails. By continuing south on SR 49 to East Glacier Park you'll come to another short spur road leading back into Glacier. This is the Two Medicine Valley area. Less developed than the area along the Going to the Sun Road, this region features one of Glacier's deepest and most beautiful valleys, the Two Medicine Lake and a trail to the Twin Falls.

It takes almost an entire day to visit Glacier National Park, just for the Going to the Sun Road and Many Glacier regions. It would be best to allow almost two days if your visit is going to be a more comprehensive one, including Waterton Lakes. It is, without a doubt, time well spent.

From East Glacier Park, where additional accommodations are available, (also, see the side trips section later) take US 2 east to the town of Browning. The community is the economic and administrative center for the Blackfeet Indian Reservation. The **Museum of the Plains Indian**, located at the intersection of US Routes 2 and 89, is one of the finest museums devoted to the history and culture of the native North Americans of the Great Plains. The comprehensive exhibits and artifacts require a minimum of one hour to be properly digested.

Leaving Browning via US 89 south, it's an easy 69-mile drive to the town of Choteau. The small **Old Trail Museum** is devoted mainly to local history, but there's an interesting exhibit on the discovery of dinosaur bones in the vicinity. The brief stop is just past the midway point between Browning and your next major destination, the city of Great Falls. US 89 runs into I-15 about 10 miles north of the city. Exit at Central Avenue and follow that east for two miles to 13th Street. Take a left on that street until you reach the **C. M. Russell Museum**. The main structure of the complex is an attractive modern gallery designed to house the works of this noted artist of the American West. It's perhaps the largest collection of his works assembled in one place, although he was so prolific that it's hard to tell; other places make the same claim. The bright and spacious gallery also has many of Russell's personal documents. On the grounds you'll also find the Charles Russell Home and Studio in adjacent wooden buildings. The studio is especially interesting as it contains many of the artist's work tools, including paint brushes, as well as artifacts that he used as subjects in his paintings. The attractive grounds contain a sculpture of the artist. It takes between 60 and 90 minutes minimum to tour the complex, even longer if you intend to linger and admire the paintings.

East of downtown via 2nd Avenue is the **Malstrom Air Force Base Museum and Air Park**. The building houses a collection of photographs, uniforms, documents and other items that describe the history of the base and its role in protecting the nation. The outdoor park has both aircraft and missiles, mostly post-World War II vintage. Allow about 45 minutes for both sections.

Located on River Drive along the Missouri River in the northeastern corner of the city is the **Giant Springs Fish, Wildlife and Parks Visitor Center and Fish Hatchery**. (Please hold for a moment while we check to see if this wins the title of "longest named attraction in the book.") While the falls of Great Falls may no longer be so great due to construction of dams, the Giant Springs is one of the largest in existence with a daily flow of almost 400 million gallons at a constant temperature of 54°. From a platform at the lake's edge you can view the crystal clear waters emerging from the spring. The park also contains scenic overlooks of the Missouri River as well as exhibits on wildlife. A visitor center contains information about the springs along with activities and sights within the park. The fish hatchery is open to the public – trout and salmon are raised here. Give yourself about an hour to visit the Giant Springs.

Great Falls has many different motels to choose from, including members of the Best Western, Comfort and Holiday Inn chains. There's also a major shopping center (almost 100 stores) located off I-15 on 10th Avenue.

Leave Great Falls by taking I-15 south. The road provides pleasant scenery as it's flanked by the Helena and Lewis & Clark National Forests. A couple of miles west of Exit 270 is the **Ulm Pushkin State Monument**. This is another example of an Indian buffalo jump, and features a 50-foot-high cliff where the Indians forced the buffalo to jump to their deaths. The cliffs contain many small caves. Continue on I-15 until Exit 209, about an hour's drive from Ulm Pushkin. This exit leads to the access road for the Wolf Creek area of the Helena National Forest and the forest's most scenic spot – the **Gates of the Mountains Recreation Area**. The area can be explored by hiking and by private boat. The easiest way to see everything is to take the two-hour narrated boat ride on the Missouri River. You'll pass through a canyon flanked by colorful limestone cliffs rising as much as 1,200 feet above the river. A stop is also made where you can take an easy stroll along a boardwalk and short trail into the dark and forbidding Meriwether Canyon. Oh yes, the name – Gates of the Mountains – refers to a trick that your eyes will play on you. As you cruise down the river it appears that you are coming to a dead end against the mountains; then, suddenly, a turn in the river makes it appear that the mountains themselves are opening up and letting you sail through! That's another advantage of visiting the area by boat, as only from the river itself can the "gates" be clearly seen.

From Gates of the Mountains it is less than 20 miles via the Interstate to the state capital of Helena. Once another of Montana's rough and tumble mining towns, Helena today is an attractive community dominated by the business of state government, with a heavy helping of tourism thrown in for good measure. Your first stop should be the **Cathedral of St. Helena**, downtown on Lawrence Street. The large neo-gothic structure is patterned after the Votive Church of Vienna. Its interior is richly decorated with beautiful Carrara marble and stained glass windows. Such large-scale traditional cathedral architecture is rather unusual for this part of the country. Nearby is the **Original Governor's Mansion**, built in 1888 and furnished today as it was in that time. The Victorian structure was last used as the Governor's home in 1959. Thirty-minute guided tours are given.

The current **Montana State Capitol** building is located at 6th and Montana Streets. Materials from within Montana were used almost exclusively in its construction – sandstone for the exterior and copper, of course, for the huge dome. The interior of this 1902 edifice is impressively adorned with paintings depicting aspects of Montana history, including the largest work ever commissioned by Charles M. Russell, which measures 25 feet in length. Many statues of important persons in Montana history also adorn the halls and rotunda. You can walk around on your own, but it's best to take one of the 30-minute guided tours.

Across the street from the Capitol is the **Montana Historical Society, Museum, Library and Archives** (okay, this time we won't say anything about lengthy names), one of the best museums of its type in the northern Rockies. Besides a huge collection of Western art, sculpture and photography (including many works by Russell), there are interesting exhibits that chart the course of history in Montana from prehistoric times on. Allow between 45 minutes and an hour for your visit. Departing hourly from in front of the museum is the **Last Chance Gulch Tour**, an hour-long narrated tour of the historic points of interest in Helena on a tram somewhat disguised as an old mining train. Many interesting anecdotes and little known tales are told by the informed guides. The "train" doesn't make any stops and you might want to come back to explore the historic areas further on your own. One such area in particular is **Reeders Alley** (off of Park Avenue), which was once the home of miners and Chinese laborers, but is now comprised mostly of chic speciality shops.

For those willing to make a 15-mile side trip in return for an interesting bit of history and some spectacular scenery, **Frontier Town** is the ideal solution. Located at the MacDonald Pass on US 12, Frontier Town sits right on the Continental Divide! You'll have a panorama of almost 100 miles of Big Sky Country. The town itself is a recreation of a pioneer settlement where you can explore a number of buildings furnished in period. There's also a museum. Including the time to and from Helena, allow about two hours.

Helena, too, has plenty of accommodations. Budget chains such as EconoLodge and Super 8 are in vogue here, along with some higher-priced hotels. There's a member of the 4B's chain for dining and one place we especially like is the Frontier Pies Restaurant and Bakery. Forget the food, which is good – you'll love the variety of fresh baked pies for desert or to go, in case you want something to munch on during a quiet evening in a Helena motel.

Take US 287 south from Helena for 32 miles to the town of Townsend where you can make a brief rest stop at another local history museum, this one called the **Broadwater County Museum**. If you have a little extra time you can take a 20-mile detour to the east of Townsend on US 12 along the **Deep Creek Canyon Drive**. This area is one of the most scenic portions of the Helena National Forest. There are numerous pull outs for taking in the mountain scenery and access to densely wooded trails. Wildlife abounds here and there's a good chance that you'll spot at least a few deer and elk. Allow about 90 minutes for this attraction, including travel time but not counting any hikes. After returning to Townsend continue south on US 287 for 31 miles until you reach I-90, in the vicinity of the Three Forks. Now you'll be returning on the Interstate toward Billings, traversing the same stretch of highway as you did at the beginning of our Montana journey. Should you want to break up the ride, you can do some of the sights we included earlier on the way back instead. It's a fair distance to Billings, but on the high speed Interstate it can be accomplished in about three hours.

The trip is not, however, complete when you get back to Billings. Seven miles southeast of town (towards the Crow Indian Reservation) is the **Pictographs Cave State Monument**. The site consists of two small caverns that were homes to Native Americans for centuries before the arrival of Europeans on the scene. One of the cave walls is covered with drawings made by the inhabitants. Largely sheltered from the effects of weather and erosion, many of the drawings are in remarkably good condition. Head back to I-90 after your brief visit to the caves and take it eastbound once again. The community of Hardin, on the edge of the huge Crow Indian Reservation, is an important center for the reservation's economic and cultural activities. Hardin has an annual reenactment of Custer's Last Stand on the weekend closest to June 25th and it's worth arranging your visit for this time if at all possible. Continue on I-90 to the US 212 exit and go a half-mile east to the **Little Bighorn Battlefield National Monument** (formerly called the Custer Battlefield). The monument describes and commemorates the events in 1876 that culminated in the most famous engagement of all the Indian Wars, the annihilation of the 7th Cavalry Regiment under George Custer by the Sioux and Northern Cheyenne. A large visitor center tells the story through photographs, maps and dioramas. You can walk out on the battlefield site by easy trail. Allow about an hour.

After making your own last stand at Little Bighorn, go back to Hardin and take County Route 313 south into the **Bighorn Canyon National Recreation Area.** You may recall that this area was described in the Wyoming chapter, but that portion of Bighorn Canyon could not be seen from the Montana side. Likewise, what we describe here can only be seen from Montana. The gorgeous canyon runs for 71 miles and is surrounded by towering cliffs. The headquarters for the area is in Fort Smith, 44 miles south of Hardin. There's a visitor center describing recreational activities (mainly boating, fishing and water sports), as well as focussing on the wildlife and native peoples of the area. The Yellowtail Dam Visitor Center has guided tours of the high dam and great views of the canyon and its sheer walls that rise almost a half-mile above the water. This is probably the most scenic portion of the entire recreation area. It may not be one of America's best known scenic places, but it certainly compares favorably with its more famous brethren. Allow approximately 2½ hours for visiting Bighorn Canyon (exclusive of any recreational activities). This includes the nearly 30 miles that you'll be driving within the recreation area.

Retrace your route back to Hardin and then on to Billings once again. However, this time it's for good as we've reached the end of our loop through the Big Sky Country.

Alternative Routes

This section of the chapter again enables readers to add more and different sights by taking alternative or side trips from the main route. Note that a section of Montana south of Missoula is included in the chapter on Idaho because of highway logistics. Roads don't always follow the lines we draw as borders. We'll discuss the one alternative route first.

The Yellowstone Option

Our alternative route is intended for those who won't be visiting Wyoming but want to see Yellowstone National Park. The park's proximity to Montana (only a very small portion of its western and northern edge actually lie within Montana), makes it an excellent addition to any Montana trip.

This route deviates from the suggested main itinerary shortly after leaving Billings. At the town of Laurel, 16 miles west of Billings along I-90, take US 212 westbound. This extraordinarily beautiful route is known as the **Beartooth Scenic Highway**. Although the entire stretch is picturesque, the best part begins after the town of Red Lodge. Before leaving town you can make a brief stop at the local **Carbon County Historical Museum**. Red Lodge is also a year-round outdoor sports center and, as such, the locale for many motels and resorts.

The lowest elevation on the Beartooth Highway is a lofty 5,650 feet, but it reaches 10,947 feet at Beartooth Pass as you cross the Wyoming line. The highway has, fortunately, been constructed with many overlooks so you can safely admire the magnificent scenery. There are places where you'll have views extending 50 miles or more. Mountains and forests dominate, but there are beautiful glaciers throughout the year, too. (The road is open from May through September, subject to late and early winter storms.) You'll also see many lovely waterfalls and unusual rock formations. A section of the road lies in Wyoming, but you cross back into Montana after traversing the Colter Pass. Here you'll reach Cooke City, which is only four miles from the northeast entrance to Yellowstone. The **Yellowstone Wildlife Museum** displays over 100 animals both large and small that are native to the area. Accommodations are available both in Cooke City and in the adjacent town of Silver Gate.

Use the information in the Wyoming chapter to construct your tour of Yellowstone via the Grand Loop Road. The loop will make its way from Tower Junction to Mammoth Hot Springs. At that point you can leave the park via the North entrance at the town of Gardiner, Montana. (An even longer alternative would add Grand Teton.) From the North entrance of Yellowstone at Gardiner it's 53 miles back to the main route at Livingston via scenic US 89. Mountains and forest again dominate the view, but there is an unusual rock formation known as the Devil's Slide about five miles north of Gardiner.

This alternative route adds approximately 240 miles to the main route, including 150 miles along Yellowstone's Grand Loop Road. It is all along highly scenic routes – the Beartooth Scenic Highway and along US 89 through Paradise Valley.

Other Side Trips

Billings to Pompeys Pillar

This short excursion, 60 miles round trip from Billings, goes to the **Pompeys Pillar National Historic Lewis and Clark Landmark**. The pillar is a tall sandstone formation and a prominent landmark that rises from the relatively flat surrounding terrain and was used by pioneers to chart their way. Lewis and Clark were the first to recognize its value as a trailblazer and Mr. Clark couldn't resist the temptation to carve his name into the rock. His early graffiti was followed by many other settlers on their westward trek. Allow about 2½ hours for the round trip.

To the Ninemile Divide

This is another 60-mile round trip, but it departs from and returns to Missoula. Use I-90 westbound from Missoula for 25 miles to Exit 82. Head north to the **Ninemile Remount Depot and Ranger Station**. The station is home to forest ranger fire fighters on a ranch spread over more than 5,000 acres. Some of the buildings are historic and reflect the daily routine of the fire fighters in the early and middle of the 20th century. Those who are interested can wander through the buildings. To the immediate north of the station are the **Grand Menard Discovery Trails**, two short trails (each less than a mile) that loop through a pine forest. The scenery on the way to Ninemile Remount and at the site itself is very picturesque. Nearby are several ghost mining towns, with Stark being the easiest to get to. Follow signs for Stark from the Interstate. The total excursion from Missoula should take less than four hours. Some of the Missoula attractions on the main itinerary are already west of the city, so you can shorten this side trip by 10 miles. If you don't need to return to Missoula and head north on US 93 instead, the trip will only cover about 50 miles.

Whitefish Country

This excursion gives you the choice between a short or long tour. The shorter option leaves the main route at Kalispell and rejoins it 18 miles further along at Columbia Falls on the way to Glacier National Park. It adds only 25 miles to the main itinerary. Take US 93 north from Kalispell to Whitefish. The town lies at the southern end of Whitefish Lake, another mountain-rimmed beauty that provides year round recreational opportunities and is a sheer pleasure to admire. The **Big Mountain Ski and Summer Resort** is eight miles further north. Summer visitors will want to take the gondola to the top of The Big Mountain, which has an altitude of 6,770 feet. It's not the biggest mountain around, despite the name, but still provides a wonderful view of the surrounding terrain, including portions of Glacier National Park. You can even see into Canada. Carriage rides are available at the park-like summit. After returning to Whitefish, rejoin the main route by taking SR 40 to Columbia Falls and pick up US 2. The entire round trip should take approximately 2½ hours, unless you wish to spend a lot of time hiking on Big Mountain.

The longer version also leaves from Kalispell, but covers approximately 225 miles before returning to Kalispell. It requires an entire day. If you didn't spend the previous night in Whitefish, you'll need a place to stay on this route and the best choice is the town of Libby, which lies approximately half-way through this extended side trip. While the number of specific attractions may be low in Montana's northeastern corner, the scenic beauty is high in this land of lofty mountains, deep valleys, forests, lakes and rivers. The journey continues north on US 93 after the Big Mountain Resort area.

The town of Eureka, 53 miles north of Whitefish and seven miles south of the Canadian border, has a local history museum called the **Tobacco Valley Historical Museum.** Once past the town follow signs for the **Ten Lakes Scenic Area**. This region, adjacent to Canada, has numerous trails of varying lengths and difficulty that afford spectacular views of the mountain lakes. While most of the trails are long and intended for overnight backpackers, some are short enough to be part of this day trip. More detailed information is available from the supervisor of the Flathead National Forest. Proceed south on SR 37 (the junction is about a mile north of Eureka) and you'll enter the Kootenai National Forest. This vast land covers almost 2¼ million acres and is dominated by craggy mountains. There is a great deal of wildlife – bald eagles inhabit the area in large numbers all year round. The road hugs the eastern shore of Lake Koocanusa, a 90-mile impoundment of the Kootenay River created by the construction of the Libby Dam. It's an unusual lake in that it is very narrow, averaging about two miles, which isn't much more than the Kootenay River without the dam. Thus, many visitors don't realize that it's a lake at all. Whether you call it a lake or river doesn't matter; the deep blue water running through a rugged mountain gorge is a beautiful sight. There are numerous places along the route to stop for a better look or to have a picnic lunch. At **Libby Dam** there's a visitor center and a scenic vista where you get a great view from the top of the 420-foot-high dam that stretches across a 2,900-foot-long crest.

Continue on SR 37 for another 17 miles into Libby. The town is the center of the area's recreational pursuits which include fishing, boating, rafting and other outdoor activities. The **Heritage Museum** is an odd 12-sided log structure that depicts regional history and the three most important influences upon the development of Libby – fur trapping, mining and lumbering.

Upon leaving Libby head east on US 2 which will bring you back to Kalispell after a 90-mile journey through more mountain valleys, forests and lakes. Thompson and McGregor Lakes, lying along the roadside, are especially picturesque. One last stop just before reaching Kalispell (four miles southwest of town via Foyes Lake Road) is the **Lone Pine State Park**. The park has several easy walks through pine forests as well as a visitor center, but the most important feature is the stunning vista of the broad Flathead Valley that's available from an easily reached overlook.

Along the Flathead River

This route traverses a portion of US 2 along the southern border of Glacier National Park. It's a most beautiful byway stretching from West Glacier to East Glacier, but one that isn't seen by many tourists. However, it's worth journeying a few extra miles to cover at least part of this route which parallels the Middle Fork of the Flathead River. The distance between West and East Glacier is 56 miles each way. The most scenic portion is the 35-mile stretch beginning at East Glacier Park and extending through the Marias Pass (elevation 5,216 feet) and just past where the road turns sharply until you finally reach the small town of Essex. There are views of the rugged and glacier-covered mountains of the park to your north and the thick tree-covered mountains of the Flathead National Forest to the south of the road. Wildlife abounds, especially mountain goats and bighorn sheep, which are often seen clinging to the rocky slopes above the road. There are several overlooks along US 2. You should figure on spending about three hours for the almost 70-mile round trip, and as much as five hours if you decide to go all the way to West Glacier. Those who add on the additional 40-odd miles from Essex to West Glacier and back will be amply rewarded with more beautiful scenery on both sides of the road. Remember that the road parallels a part of the river that is traversed by many of the float trips leaving from West Glacier. Readers who already took this river journey would probably find this side trip redundant.

A Final Round-Up

It doesn't take a genius to look at the map of Montana and realize that a substantial portion of the state (namely, the eastern section) hasn't been covered in the routes above. As we've already mentioned, Montana is just too big to cover entirely in one trip unless you're going to be spending months away from home. The eastern portion of the state has fewer attractions and far less outstanding scenery than do the areas that we've covered. However, that doesn't mean there isn't anything to see. Other opportunities abound for those readers who'll be driving into Montana from the upper Midwest, which means arriving in Montana via I-94. The following section lists, in order from east to west, the sights on or near I-94 from the North Dakota border to Billings. The Interstate parallels the Yellowstone River for almost 200 miles from the town of Glendive to the junction of I-90 near Billings. There are several state recreation areas offering activities and picnicking scattered along this section of the highway.

Glendive offers, in town, via Exit 215 off of I-94, the **Frontier Gateway Museum**. Exhibits range from geology displays to several frontier buildings that have been reconstructed on the site. The **Makoshika State Park** is three miles south of Glendive via County Route 335. The name is an Indian word meaning "bad lands." The vast tract of badlands formations begins south of Badlands National Park in South Dakota, skirts the edge of the Black Hills and then runs north along both the South and North Dakota borders into Wyoming and, finally, covers the southeastern portion of Montana. The section in Makoshika State Park covers 8,100 acres and is highlighted by very colorful buttes, odd rock formations created by erosion. Deep gullies filled with a variety of colors are also characteristic of the area. Two separate nature trails provide easy access to most of the sights and there is an interesting visitor center with many fossil samples. Fossils are commonly found throughout the western badlands. Allow a minimum of two hours to visit Makoshika, including hiking both trails.

Forty miles further along I-90 in the small town of Terry is the **Prairie County Museum**, notable because it is located in a bank building dating from 1915. Then it's 36 more miles to the next major town, Miles City.

Miles City has a municipal park located on the Yellowstone River and there is a scenic overlook. The **Range Riders Museum and Bert Clark Gun Collection**, on the I-94 business loop, features exhibits on geology and archaeology as well as frontier history. Miles City began as Fort Keogh in 1877, an outpost active in the Indian Wars. Part of the original officers' quarters are on the grounds of the multi-building complex. More than 500 different types of firearms are contained in the gun collection. Allow approximately 75 minutes. The last stop on the way into Billings is in Pompeys Pillar, which was previously described in one of the side trips.

If you're not driving into Montana by I-94 the journey from Billings to Glendive and back again is approximately 420 miles, slightly less if you already went as far as Pompeys Pillar. Travel time plus time for the attractions would probably mean adding two full days to your trip. We can't enthusiastically recommend adding that much driving for what you're going to see, especially if you've already seen Badlands National Park.

Chapter 3

Idaho

The Secret Beauty

There is probably no other state in the United States that is subject
to so much misunderstanding by a majority of Americans than
Idaho. Most of us, except for residents of Idaho and those who
have traveled through its many memorable sights, vaguely recall
seeing Idaho on the map. We remember the narrow northern
panhandle and think of Idaho as a rather small, skinny piece of
land. In fact, it is the 11th largest state. Aside from some skiing
enthusiasts who know about Sun Valley, just about everyone
knows Idaho for its famous potatoes and many people think of it
as open farm land. Here, too, nothing could be further from the
truth. For while there is much fertile farm land to grow potatoes
and scores of other crops, Idaho is a land of breathtaking contrasts.
From the rushing Snake River winding its way through awesome
Hell's Canyon, to the majestic mountains of the Sawtooth National Recreation Area, to the unreal landscape of Craters of the
Moon, Idaho is a land of diverse beauty. We hope that after
reading this chapter you'll appreciate all of the many worthwhile
attractions that make Idaho an exciting vacation destination.

Along the Suggested Itinerary

Because of its small population, Idaho doesn't have the greatest
air connections. Nonetheless, there are two good gateways. The
first is Boise, the state capital and largest city in the three states
covered in this volume. As such, that's where we'll begin our tour.
However, many travelers will find it more convenient to fly into
Spokane, Washington, which is less than 40 miles from the Idaho
border. Those who take this second option can take US 195 south
for 110 miles to Lewiston and pick up the main itinerary. If you're
taking the Panhandle alternative routing (see next section), then
it's only 50 miles east on I-90 from Spokane's airport to the Idaho

town of Coeur d'Alene. If you're driving into Idaho from the west you'll be using either I-90 from Spokane or I-84 which joins the route as soon as it crosses the Oregon-Idaho border. From the south or east I-15 and I-84 link up with the main route either at Pocatello (I-15) or near Burley along I-84.

Boise, with a population of approximately 130,000, is the only place in Idaho that truly deserves the "city" status. The state's other settlements are little more than towns, albeit some of large. The name comes from the river running through the city which, in French, meant "wooded." The name is appropriate, for Boise lies in a beautiful valley setting of forests and mountains. It is spared much of the extreme heat and cold that is the rule in most other areas of the state; perhaps that is one of the reasons why so many people have settled here and in neighboring communities to the east and west.

From the airport, Vista Avenue runs north into Capitol Boulevard and downtown. On I-84 use Exits 49 or 54 for the quickest access into the city center. The Boise River bisects the city, running from the northwest corner to the southeast. Most sights are north of the river. Getting around town is easy, although few attractions are concentrated in the downtown walking area. As a result, a car is necessary to take in all the sights of the capital city. Compared to most cities, you'll find the traffic light and negotiating city streets to be a simple task. A visitor information bureau is located at 100 N. 9th Street in the heart of downtown. The helpful staff will be glad to provide you with information on sightseeing, lodging, dining and other activities.

The northern part of the city is roughly bisected by Capitol Blvd., which runs from the Boise River. Between 6th and 8th Streets is the **Idaho State Capitol**. Although construction began in 1905 the structure wasn't completed until 1920. Patterned after the US Capitol and built primarily with local sandstone (although marble comes from several states), your visit to the Capitol will be most enjoyable if you take one of the guided tours. The lobby has exhibits on Idaho's mineral and agricultural wealth. Be sure to take note of the five-foot-high golden eagle that graces the Capitol's dome. There are several historic monuments and statues on the grounds.

Three blocks to the northwest, at 11th and Franklin, is the **First United Methodist Church**. More commonly known as the Cathedral of the Rockies, the gothic-style structure is noted for its fine stained glass windows.

Still downtown, the **Discovery Center of Idaho** (131 W. Myrtle Street) is a science museum that teaches through participation. Almost 100 hands-on exhibits will entertain both children and adults. A completely different experience awaits visitors at the nearby world headquarters of **Boise-Cascade Corporation** (954 Jefferson). The attractive building contains a large atrium in which you can walk through a virtual indoor forest. The corporate public relations moguls like to emphasize Boise-Cascade's responsible environmental record. True or not, they've done a fine job here. The historic center of Boise is in an area bordered by Main and Grove Streets between 5th and 10th Streets. Many buildings here date from the mid to late 19th century. If you're especially interested in this type of walking tour, the visitor information bureau can outline further details for you.

Stretching for almost a mile along the north shore of the Boise River, within a short walking distance from the Capitol, is **Julia Davis Park**. One of many attractive green areas in the "City of Trees," this tranquil oasis is important to visitors because it houses some of Boise's best museums and other attractions. These include the adjacent **Idaho Historical Museum** and the **Boise Art Museum**. The former chronicles the history of the state through exhibits and artifacts while the latter boasts a number of changing exhibits in addition to its own permanent collection. **Zoo Boise** provides an interesting alternative to the usual municipal zoo that you're probably accustomed to. Although you'll find a petting zoo, the highlight here is the large collection of birds of prey, one of the largest of its type in the nation. A final attraction is the attractive rose garden. It will take close to two hours to explore the park's facilities adequately, longer if you look at everything in detail.

One last item that begins at Julia Davis Park, but isn't actually located within it's 90-odd acres, is the **Boise Tour Train**. Running only in the summer, the open-air cars are pulled by a vehicle made to resemble a late 19th-century steam engine. This hour-long narrated tour is a good way to take in the sights of the historic and downtown areas of Boise.

Heading east from downtown, Main Street turns into Warm Springs Road. Less than three miles from the city center is the **Old Idaho Penitentiary**. When the prison was shut in 1973, having been in use for over 100 years, it was turned into a museum. Many exhibits on criminal activity and prison life are in the complex of buildings, which are surrounded by massive sandstone walls. The garden area is maintained in the manner it was by prisoners at the turn of the century. You'll be able to visit Death Row, the gallows and the harsh solitary confinement areas. Some buildings have been converted to use as museums on topics unrelated to prison life, such as the **Idaho Transportation Museum** and a museum on the history of electricity in Idaho. Allow at least one hour to tour the entire complex. Just outside the prison walls are the **Idaho Botanical Gardens**. The gardens feature seven separate areas, including herb and children's gardens. Perhaps the most interesting is a section with large fragrant flowers especially grown to attract butterflies and hummingbirds, two fascinating groups of species. Hummingbirds are extremely quick and spotting them calls for a sharp eye and patience, but the beautiful tiny creatures are worth a little work. There's also a nature trail of less than a mile that winds through the foothills surrounding Boise. Most visitors will need at least an hour to explore the gardens.

The remainder of Boise's attractions are scattered around the city, but none of them are more than a 20-minute ride from downtown. The **Morrison Knudsen Nature Center** (600 S. Walnut) was developed by the large and well known Morrison Knudsen engineering and construction firm. The center is an outstanding example of how natural ecosystems can be reproduced and maintained, allowing visitors to experience them first hand. Several types of terrain and many different animal habitats will be found along the attractive pathways that meander through the preserve. This is another attraction that deserves an hour of your time.

The campus of **Boise State University**, across the river from Julia Davis Park, contains several exhibits that might be of interest to political historians, including the papers of the influential Idaho Senator, Frank Church, and a center devoted to Western Studies.

About seven miles south of Boise via Cole Road (I-84, Exit 50) is the wonderful **World Center for Birds of Prey**. The purpose of the center is to protect, preserve and promote the growth of endangered bird species, including eagles, hawks and falcons. Tours of the center allow visitors to view incubators where the birds are hatched and cared for until they're capable of making it on their own and are released into the wild. Reservations are required for the hour-long tours and can be made by calling (208) 362-3716. Late spring to mid-summer is the best time to visit. The center is located near to the Snake River Birds of Prey Natural Area. If you're interested in visiting this more remote and harder to reach area, further information can be obtained at the center.

Finally, Boise is home to a major forest fire fighting center, the **Boise Interagency Fire Center**. Advance reservations are required for tours that take you through the center and explain the equipment that is used to detect, monitor and fight forest fires. Call (208) 389-2512 for information on tour times and directions. Availability is often limited.

Boise Odds & Ends: As Idaho's largest city, it has a wide choice of accommodations. Many major chains are represented, primarily in the budget and moderate price ranges. A room in Boise will set your pocketbook back less than in most places. Hotels and motels are located throughout the city, but concentrated along the I-84 corridor, especially near the airport to the south of downtown. While not known as a gourmet town, it's still large enough to find food of practically every variety. Some good places for a quick lunch can be found clustered in the Eighth Street Marketplace.

Theater and ballet are among Boise's cultural pursuits. If you're interested, contact the visitor information bureau. Recreation and relaxation opportunities abound. The many city parks are a good choice, including **Veterans Memorial State Park** and **Lucky Peak State Park**. The former, in addition to miles of trails and picnic areas, has a lake for fishing. Lucky Peak has a swimming area. Children, and even some adults, will find the **Wild Waters Waterslide Theme Park**, just off the Cole Road exit of I-84, a good spot to unwind.

While Boise is both an interesting and scenic city, like all of the western states, your true outdoor experience doesn't begin until you get out of town. So now is a good time to begin the journey through Idaho's many wonders.

Just west of Boise along I-84 are the adjacent communities of Nampa and Caldwell. With a combined population of almost 50,000, the Nampa-Caldwell area ranks as one of Idaho's most "crowded." A number of excursions to former mining towns can be made from Nampa and are detailed in the side-trips section later in this chapter. Nampa's highlight is the **Deer Flat National Wildlife Refuge**. Only the Lake Lowell section, located four miles southwest of town, is readily accessible. Waterfowl and animals are contained within the refuge, but in order to protect them, visitation in the winter months is often restricted. But there's plenty of activity all year, so don't skip this opportunity to admire nature. A mile-long nature trail is the best way to get a close-up view of the birds and small animals. Swimming is available. Within the town of Nampa is the **Canyon County Historical Museum**, one of many local history exhibits you'll encounter throughout Idaho. Caldwell is known as the wine capital of Idaho and a number of wineries can be visited. The most popular is the **Ste. Chapelle Winery**, reached by taking SR 55 southwest for eight miles and then following signs for another half-mile. Tours and tastings are offered and jazz music performances are added on Sunday from mid-June to late July. Allow at least a half-hour. Food and lodging are plentiful throughout the Nampa-Caldwell area.

Continue west on I-84 for just under 30 miles to the Payette exit and pick up US 95 northbound for the short ride into town. The **Payette County Historical Society Museum** is located here. Ten miles further north is the community of Weiser. This attractive town on the Snake River features many stately homes in the Queen Anne style and a local history museum. Another 31 miles north on US 95 brings you to the town of Cambridge. This town is one of the gateways into the wonderfully scenic Hells Canyon and Seven Devils areas. Heading north via SR 71 from Cambridge provides the easiest road access into the **Hells Canyon National Recreation Area**. An alternative route into the canyon, on one of the ever popular jet boat tours from Lewiston, is discussed later.

The round trip via SR 71 (since it dead-ends at Hells Canyon) is about 100 miles. It can be left off the main itinerary if you wish to see Hell's Canyon entirely by boat, which is the most popular method. The only problem is that you'll miss some great scenery and an exciting ride! This route enters the southern portion of the recreation area, actually crossing for a short time into Oregon. The Snake River forms the boundary between Idaho and Oregon, with the scenery on both sides being nothing short of spectacular. About half-way through the inbound trip you'll reach the town of Oxbow and the Oxbow Dam. The road ends at the Hells Canyon Dam. To your right, on the Idaho side, are great views of the rugged Seven Devils Mountains. From the dam you can also peer into the heart of Hells Canyon and admire the deep gorge. Jet boat and other water excursions are available from the town of Oxbow on the Oregon side of the border. The scenery is different than seen on water-borne excursions from Lewiston. Visiting via raft

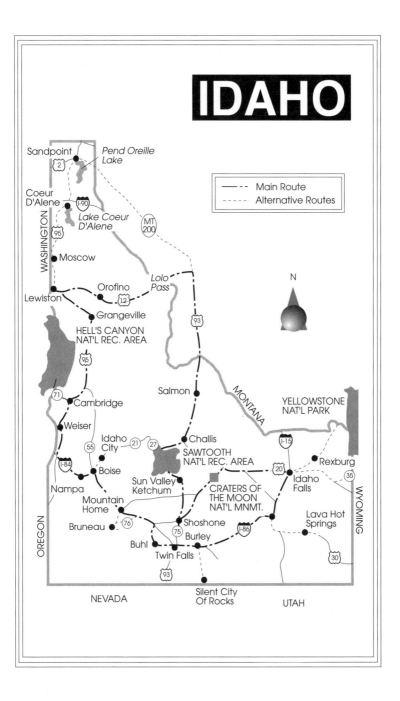

IDAHO

Main Route
Alternative Routes

Sandpoint
Pend Oreille Lake
2

Coeur D'Alene
I-90

WASHINGTON

Lake Coeur D'Alene

MT 200

Moscow

Orofino
12
Lolo Pass

Lewiston

US 93

Grangeville

HELL'S CANYON NAT'L REC. AREA

N

95

MONTANA

71
Cambridge
Salmon

YELLOWSTONE NAT'L PARK

Weiser

Idaho City
21   27
Challis

I-15

55

SAWTOOTH NAT'L REC. AREA

Rexburg
35

I-84
Boise

20
Idaho Falls

WYOMING

Nampa

Sun Valley Ketchum

CRATERS OF THE MOON NAT'L MNMT.

Mountain Home

76
Shoshone
75
Burley
I-86
Lava Hot Springs

Bruneau

Buhl
30

Twin Falls
93

OREGON

NEVADA

Silent City Of Rocks

UTAH

or jet boat from Lewiston is an absolute *must*, but the scenery encountered via the SR 71 route *cannot* be seen from the water and is, therefore, a worthwhile excursion as well. Even though SR 71 is paved, there are some hairpin turns and steep grades that you may wish to avoid. To visit this part of Hell's Canyon requires about four hours, including the round trip travel time from Cambridge, but not allowing time for a boat ride.

We should mention here that at the town of Council (23 miles north of Cambridge) you can pick up a graded road that provides access to the Seven Devils Mountains themselves as well as other portions of the recreation area. Known as the Kleinschmidt Grade, this road is *only* for the adventurous and four-wheel-drive is certainly recommended. Those who aren't intimidated by steep, winding roads at the edge of precipitous cliffs will be amply rewarded with the rugged scenery of the Hells Canyon area.

Continuing north on US 95 from Council, a pleasant 25-mile ride brings you to the town of New Meadows where accommodations are offered. A brief stop can be made at **Packer John State Park**, named for an individual who transported supplies for the miners from Lewiston to Boise back in the early 1860s.

The 80-mile section of US 95 between New Meadows and Grangeville parallels the Salmon and Little Salmon Rivers and affords many scenic vistas. Several rest areas along the way allow you to safely stop and take a closer look. To the west lies the Seven Devils Mountains while the heavily forested slopes within the Payette and Nezperce National Forests can be seen to the east. This area provides access to a number of wilderness areas for those who like their scenery while truly roughing it (information is available from the Forest Service office in Grangeville). The town of Riggins, about half-way along this stretch of US 95, is the site of the **Rapid River Salmon Hatchery**. Chinook salmon are hatched here to make up for the lower runs that result from dams on nearby rivers. Early summer is the best time to visit. Riggins lies in one of the most picturesque areas of the gorge. It is a popular spot to venture out on river trips that range from relaxing float trips to wild whitewater adventures. Trips run from a half-day to overnight in length. Grangeville is the best place for accommodations nearby.

It's another 75 miles from Grangeville to Lewiston along US 95. The less than two-hour ride continues through nice scenery, although not up to the standards that were set along the Salmon

River gorge. Lewiston has a population of almost 30,000 and has a half-dozen good motels to choose from. It's situated right on the border with Oregon. Named for the famous leaders of the Lewis and Clark expedition, the sister city of Clarkston is on the Oregon side of the border. There are some worthwhile attractions within the city, although its main claim to fame comes with its status as the water gateway to Hell's Canyon.

The town is attractively situated at the confluence of the Snake and Clearwater Rivers. The **Lewis and Clark Interpretive Center**, located where the rivers meet, commemorates the passage of the Lewis and Clark Expedition at this sight on October 10, 1805. The center lies along a paved pathway called the **Lewiston Levee Parkway**. It flanks both rivers and provides a leisurely way to stroll along the attractively landscaped waterfront. The view of the rivers and both towns from atop Lewiston Hill is wonderful. To get there, take the Spiral Highway (reached by turning left off of US 95 as soon as you cross the bridge over the Clearwater River) for about eight miles. There are some fairly steep grades and a lot of turns, but the road isn't particularly difficult.

Now we return to the matter of seeing **Hells Canyon National Recreation Area**. Hells Canyon is the nation's deepest gorge, falling just short of 8,000 feet from top to bottom at its deepest point. The *average* depth is about 5,500 feet, making the Grand Canyon seem like a gully! (Well, not really, but Idahoans can rightfully brag about their canyon, too). Of course, Hells Canyon is not nearly as wide. In fact, there are places where the river is only about 100 feet across, which makes the canyon appear even deeper. The sheer walls of a mile or more in height often stretch for several miles along the river and are an unforgettable sight. Almost 70 miles of the Snake River winds its way through the 653,000-acre recreation area. About half of the river is classified as scenic; the other half has been given the title of wild river. Day-long to two- and three-day raft trips are a leisurely and exciting way to see the area. However, as most vacationers may not have that kind of time, jet boats provide a viable alternative way of seeing the canyon. There are a number of operators in Lewiston that run these all-day trips. You'll see everything that the multi-day excursions do, just a lot quicker. Many visitors find the jet boat ride more exciting than the slower moving raft trips. The choice is yours, but be sure to have advance reservations for whichever trip you'll be taking. Consult the Addendum for information on both Hells Canyon National Recreation Area and trip outfitters, of which there are about three dozen.

While you may not want to leave Hells Canyon, we must push on with our journey. Take US 12 eastbound from Lewiston for just 11 miles to the **Nez Perce National Historic Park**. Actually, this park consists of 24 sites scattered over a wide area of north-central Idaho. All depict a portion of the history of the Nez Perce Indian tribe, and especially their struggle for freedom during the Nez Perce War that began in 1877. The park headquarters in Spalding will give visitors an understanding of their valiant fight and their accomplishments. Details on visiting other sites within the park are also available at the headquarters.

A half-hour further east on US 12 is the town of Orofino. Although small, the town is located on a major tourist route and you'll be able to find food and lodging here. Five miles before town, however, is the **Lewis and Clark Canoe Camp**, part of the Nez Perce National Historical Park. The site is where the men of the expedition camped while building the canoes that would take them on the final leg of their journey to the Pacific.

A two-mile side trip from Orofino via SR 7 will bring you to the tiny town of Ahsahka where you can visit the **Dworshak Dam** and **Dworshak National Fish Hatchery**. The dam is of a construction type called straight-axis. Don't ask us exactly what that means – but you can find out during tours of the 717-foot-high structure. It is one of the largest concrete dams of its type in the world. The hatchery produces more than five million salmon each year, also making it one of the biggest in the world. Both facilities were completed in the 1970s. The Ahsahka side trip from Orofino should take between 60 and 90 minutes. The surrounding scenery is lovely.

Continue east on US 12 from Orofino for 17 miles, past the town of Kamiah, to an unusual rock formation known as the **Heart of the Monster**. Of volcanic origin, the rock is considered to be the place of creation according to Nez Perce Indian tradition. Just beyond Kamiah in the town of Kooskia is another fish hatchery if you haven't had your fill of them already. A dozen or so miles past Kooskia US 12 enters national forest territory and begins a highly scenic run known as the **Lewis and Clark Highway Wild & Scenic River Corridor**. The name is quite a mouthful, but that's okay since the scenery is beautiful enough for you to keep your mouth open along most of the spectacular 130-mile adventure. For most of this distance there are no towns and, therefore, no food or gas, so you might want to fill up before you begin. US 12 is a good road, but it does follow a very winding course along the

Lochsa River. En route are frequent opportunities to rest at forest service campgrounds (some have trails for hiking). Heavily forested mountain slopes line both sides of the narrow river valley. At the Idaho-Montana border is the Lolo Pass (road elevation 5,233 feet). A visitor center is located at the pass. This is the site of the **Packer Meadow**, an area where many people delight in taking a walk through the colorful wildflowers. The place is ablaze with color in summer, a natural botanical garden within the confines of the Bitteroot Mountains.

Rather than back-tracking along US 12 and 95 to reach the lower eastern portion of Idaho, it's faster to travel into Montana for a brief time. Stay on US 12 until the town of Lolo (17 miles after the pass) and head south on US 93. The town of Hamilton is a good overnight stopping point. Here you can visit the **Daly Mansion**, the former home of a copper magnate. The home contains the original furnishings and is located on a 22,000-acre farm where Mr. Daly was fond of raising thoroughbred horses. About 50 miles south of Hamilton you'll cross the Chief Joseph Pass and re-enter Idaho. US 93 soon picks up the Salmon River and becomes increasingly dramatic as indicated by the name given to the highway – the **Salmon River Scenic Route**. This beautiful and primitive area is part of the Salmon National Forest. The wild river was once known as "The River of No Return" because of the hazards it presented to those trying to navigate it upstream. Power boats make today's journey much safer, but still exciting. Sections of the river are navigable to rafts and many options exist for one- to multi-day trips leaving from the town of Salmon, 45 miles south of the Montana border. Salmon, besides having a variety of lodging establishments and restaurants, is home to the **Lehmi County Historical Museum**. The museum has Indian artifacts along with exhibits on the area's booming gold-rush days in the mid-1860s.

South of Salmon US 93 continues its scenic run as it heads into the Challis National Forest and approaches the town of the same name (food and lodging are available here). From the road you'll continue to have splendid views of mountains and the Salmon River and you'll pass ghost towns and forest service visitor centers. Many mountain summits in this area exceed 10,000 feet with Mt. Borah, Idaho's highest point, being in the Challis National Forest.

Leaving Challis, US 93 heads southeast and we'll rejoin it later; but for now, head south out of town on SR 75 which will take you through one of Idaho's most beautiful sights – the **Sawtooth National Recreation Area**. There has been much talk of making the area a national park, an idea opposed by Idahoans who feel that it will bring too much development. The huge 765,000-acre area contains majestic mountain peaks (three of which are over 10,000 feet high) and several large mountain lakes. From the town of Clayton, just before you enter the recreation area, to Sun Valley, immediately south of Sawtooth, SR 75 traverses a distance of 94 highly scenic miles with plenty to see and do.

Food and accommodations are available within the recreation area in the small community of Stanley. Depending upon your schedule, you might want to wait until you reach Ketchum or Sun Valley where you'll find a much greater choice of lodging establishments. In either case, you should stop at the visitor center five miles south of Stanley to view the film on the recreation area. There are also exhibits here and you can pick up brochures that will help you decide which hiking trails and walks to try. There is also horseback riding and river rafting available in the recreation area itself. There are several short spur roads on SR 75 south of Stanley that lead to some of the stunning mountain lakes. Among the easiest of these beauties to reach are (in order, heading south) Redfish Lake, Yellow Belly Lake and Pettit Lake. A longer walk is needed to reach the latter. Good signs on the main road point the way to each destination.

SR 75 climbs slowly at first and then much more steeply as it approaches the majestic Galena Summit. On the way you should make a brief stop at the Pole Creek Ranger Station, which affords a glimpse into the early days of forest service activity. The Galena Summit Overlook, at a height of 8,752 feet, provides the most inspiring view of the Sawtooth Valley, flanked by granite peaks and filled with high meadows. Both the ascent and descent are equally breathtaking. Allow between three and four hours for visiting Sawtooth National Recreation Area, and longer if you intend to hike on any long trails.

Immediately south of Sawtooth is the Sun Valley area, world famous for some of the best skiing and winter sports available anywhere. Summertime offers other opportunities, notably for viewing the outstanding scenery. Resort prices, which are out of sight in the winter, are much more reasonable at this time of year. Whether you stay in Sun Valley or in neighboring and slightly less fashionable Ketchum, you should take some time to visit some of the Sun Valley resorts, including the Elkhorn Resort, Sun

Valley Inn and Sun Valley Lodge. Ketchum is located right on SR 75 while Sun Valley is two miles off the road. Guests at these resorts can partake in horseback riding, fishing and other leisure pursuits right on the properties. Check in at one of these major resorts if this appeals to you.

Sun Valley resembles a Swiss-style Alpine village, both in architecture and setting. It has become more sophisticated in recent years, as many art galleries now line the town's streets. Outdoor recreation opportunities abound, whether it be hiking, mountain biking, golf, tennis, soaring, or just about anything else that you can think of. The surrounding scenery makes whatever you do that much more enjoyable. Some chair lifts used to transport skiers in winter are also open at other times for those wishing to get a birds eye view of Sun Valley.

One other point of interest here is the **Ernest Hemingway Memorial**. The author loved Sun Valley, completing *For Whom The Bell Tolls* during the time when he owned a summer home here. The memorial is located along Trail Creek, which connects Ketchum and Sun Valley. In fact, an extensive trail system runs along the creek and is a good way for visitors to experience more of the area.

Continue south from Ketchum on SR 75 for 40 miles to the **Shoshone Ice Caves**. Located in an area of desolate lava beds that stretch all the way to Craters of the Moon, the Ice Caves have a year-round temperature that never goes above freezing. That can be a refreshing (but sometimes shocking) change from summer surface temperatures that are more than three times as high! Guided tours lasting almost an hour take visitors through this frozen world and explain the geological considerations that created and maintain the cave's unusual condition. Don't forget to dress appropriately; good sturdy shoes are recommended. Be aware that the tour includes many steps and would be difficult, if not impossible, for the physically challenged.

Return north on SR 75 to the junction of US 20 and head east. At the town of Carey US 20 joins US 26 and 93. Another 25 miles on the combined US 20/26/93 will bring you to one of the most unusual places, not only in Idaho, but in all of America – the **Craters of the Moon National Monument**.

Even before the Apollo astronauts used this area to train for their lunar landing mission, we were well aware that the landscape resembled that of the moon, hence the name. This 83-square-mile area contains the world's largest concentration of basaltic volcanic formations – a sea of lava fields generously sprinkled with cinder cones. The volcanic activity that created Craters of the Moon occurred between 2,000 and 15,000 years ago. The best way to see the monument is via a paved seven-mile loop drive and through some short trails. Be aware that the lava in Craters of the Moon is of the jagged type (visitors to Hawaii may recall that there's also a smooth type). It is often very sharp and can tear clothing and skin. Don't touch it and don't climb on the cinder cones. Be content to stay on the trails because you can see everything quite well from them!

Stop at the visitor center at the monument entrance to view the interesting and informative displays on the origins of the craters. The loop road takes you through an area known as the Big Craters. A short trail will take you to the top of Inferno Cone where you'll have an excellent overview of the cinder cones. Other highly visible features from the road are Big Cinder Butte and the Spatter Cones. Two other short trails lead to an area of vegetation known as the Devil's Orchard and to the Tree Mold Area where lava hardened around trees and has left an empty shell.

For the more ambitious, longer trails lead to the Cave Area. The walk to the cave takes about a half-hour each way, sometimes over rough terrain. A number of lava tubes ranging from 50 to over 800 feet in length can be explored in this area. The loop road and shorter trails can be completed in approximately two hours. Allow longer if you're visiting the Cave Area.

There aren't any decent overnight accommodations in the vicinity of the monument, so plan your schedule accordingly. Food is available in Arco, about 20 miles east on the trio of US highways. From Arco continue traveling eastbound and stay on US 20 where it splits with US 26. Take the former all the way into Idaho Falls, a distance of 67 miles from Arco. However, an interesting stop on the way, near Atomic City, is the **Experimental Breeder Reactor Number 1**. This federal laboratory has been in the forefront of research with nuclear fusion reactors. There is an interesting visitor center and guided tours can be arranged.

Idaho Falls has a population of over 45,000, making it the state's third largest city and one that has all of the dining, lodging and shopping facilities that were scarce between here and Sun Valley. The Snake River runs through the city and is flanked by a series of parks that contain most of the points of interest. The low but wide and rather turbulent **Idaho Falls** are on River Parkway, a half-mile from the Broadway exit of I-15. A greenbelt extends from the falls picnic area for over two miles. The **Idaho Falls Zoo** features large cats and other animals and is located in Taupthaus Park.

A **Mormon Temple** on Memorial Drive near the falls has lovely grounds and, like all Mormon Temples, is of interest architecturally. There is a visitor center located there but the interior of the Temple is closed to non-Mormons. One of Idaho Fall's most interesting attractions is the **Bonneville Museum** (200 N. Eastern Avenue). It traces the history of the area and includes an interesting walk through exhibits depicting life in Eagle Rock, the name that Idaho Falls went by in its early days. Allow about 45 minutes for the museum. The other attractions in town will generally take a half-hour or less.

Idaho Falls is an excellent place to link up with the Wyoming itinerary, but more about that in the section on combining journeys. For now, head south on I-15. It's only an hour drive on the interstate to your next stop, Idaho's second largest city, Pocatello. Plenty of choices are available in the lodging area, including many representatives of the largest national chains.

The city was once part of the Fort Hall Indian Reservation and still plays an important economic role for the Indians who reside on the reservation. Pocatello is also the home of Idaho State University. The two most important sites for visitors are the **Bannock County Historical Museum** and the **Fort Hall Replica**. Both are located in the Ross Park area at the southern end of the city just off of I-15. (Ross Park also contains a small zoo and a rose garden with over 1,000 rose bushes.) The Museum contains an extensive collection of artifacts related both to the area's Indians and Pocatello's important role in the Union Pacific Railroad. Allow about a half-hour. The Fort Hall Replica is authentic in every detail, except that it was relocated to be near the park. The purpose of the old fort was to protect the fur trade and you can walk through the fort's various buildings and have a good feel for how things were back in the 1830s.

A final item of interest in Pocatello is the campus of Idaho State University, which contains the **Idaho Museum of Natural History**. The focus of the museum is on the ancient animals of the area, notably dinosaurs and mammals from the ice age.

We'll leave Pocatello by heading back north on I-15 for a short time to the north edge of town and then head west on I-86 for the 22-mile drive to American Falls. The town is tucked into the southwestern corner of the American Falls Reservoir, a man-made impoundment of the Snake River. At the dam there is a visitor center and fish hatchery. You can also take a tour of the power-house. Perhaps the town's most interesting visitor attraction is the **Massacre Rocks State Park**, located five miles west. The name comes from a skirmish between settlers and Indians that occurred in the river gorge, made narrow at this point by the large rocks. Trails wind through the scenic landscape and there's a visitor center that explains the events related to the misnamed "massacre." One of the unique features of the area is a large boulder called Register Rock, so called because many settlers carved their names into the rock on their journey westward. Allow at least 45 minutes to visit the park.

More adventurous visitors can make a side trip at this point to the Great Rift and Crystal Ice Cave on very difficult and unpaved roads. If you're interested in making this excursion, inquire in the town of American Falls for directions and road conditions. Do not attempt the trip during or after heavy rain or even if bad weather is on the horizon.

Interstate 86 ends a few miles after Massacre Rocks, joining I-84 and continuing to parallel the Snake River. About 50 miles from American Falls you'll reach the town of Burley, where you can make a brief stop at the **Cassia County Historical Museum**. There are also food and accommodations available in town.

Another 50 miles on I-84 brings you to Twin Falls, the last major community on our circle route before returning to Boise. The area is now known primarily for agriculture, made possible by irrigation projects using the waters of the Snake River. The many dams that have been constructed to control flooding and facilitate agriculture have all but wiped out the two falls that gave the town its name. However, six miles northeast of town (via SR 75) are the magnificent **Shoshone Falls**. At 212 feet in height, they're 45 feet higher than Niagara and almost as wide. The falls are best viewed in spring since water diverted for summer use tends to reduce the flow. Nevertheless, it's a most impressive sight at any time.

The Twin Falls area is located in one of the most scenic portions of the Snake River Gorge. Nowhere is this more evident than in the viewing areas on and adjacent to the **Perrine Memorial Bridge** which spans the gorge. It is 486 feet above the river, making it one of the highest bridges of its type in the country. From the bridge and trail system you can see the sheer cliffs of the canyon, lakes and numerous waterfalls. A road goes down from near the bridge to the bottom of the canyon. It's steep but not especially difficult and well worth the effort. It requires about 45 minutes to take in all of the vantage points of the gorge and bridge.

Twin Falls has a large variety of accommodations. Upon leaving town, take US 30 (continuing beyond the Perrine Bridge) west. Although it roughly parallels the Interstate, this older route will provide access to a number of highly scenic and unusual attractions. Twelve miles west of the Bridge is the town of Buhl. Six miles west of town, following signs for Castleford, is the **Balanced Rock** formation. It's 40 feet high and sits precariously on a narrow base. Logic would seem to dictate that it should topple, but it hasn't and probably won't for some time (perhaps a few hundred thousand more years).

Now return to US 30, continuing westward to the **Thousand Springs**. This will bring you back into the Snake River Canyon and standing before you, for a distance of almost two miles, is an incredible panorama of natural springs gushing forth from the rocky walls. At one time there were many more than the several hundred that exist today, but the sight is still an unusual one.

A few miles further on US 30 from the Thousand Springs is the town of Hagerman, home of two significant attractions, the **Malad Gorge State Park** and the **Hagerman Fossil Beds National Landmark**. The gorge is about 250 feet deep and at one point, by the Devil's Washbowl, the canyon narrows to a scant 140 feet across. Some of the springs found in the Thousand Springs area also make an appearance here. At the Devil's Washbowl is a 60-foot-high waterfall and a wild whirlpool. The park contains a system of trails, some of which are real cliffhangers and definitely not for those with fear of high places. However, there is an excellent footbridge that spans the gorge and allows visitors easily to view the most beautiful of the park's sights. Allow 30 minutes, but much more if you'll be descending into the gorge. The Fossil Beds National Landmark preserves some of the best examples of marine and small mammal fossils found anywhere. Many of the specimens average three million years in age and are remarkably well preserved. The beds run for miles along the escarpment, which in past geologic eras was completely submerged. A visitor center explains the fossils that you'll see and puts everything into a multimillion-year perspective.

Route US 30 rejoins I-84 at Bliss, just eight miles beyond Hagerman. Exit at Glenn's Ferry to visit the **Three Island Crossing State Park**. Among the park's major stars are a small herd of Buffalo. The crossing was of importance during the westward trek on the Oregon Trail and a visitor center is here that will explain all of the important historic events.

Once you return to I-84 it's under an hour back to Boise and the completion of the main itinerary.

Alternative Routes

While the above itinerary includes a large proportion of Idaho's many attractions, there still is much more to see for those who have the time and inclination. As in the preceding chapters, alternatives to the main itinerary are presented here. The first description below is the only true alternative routing; the others are side trips varying from a few miles and a couple of hours to one that could last an additional week if you wanted.

The Panhandle Alternative Route

This routing departs from the main itinerary at Lewiston, heading north through the Idaho Panhandle, the long and narrow point at the top of the state that reaches all the way to the Canadian border, and finally rejoining the main route at the junction of US 12 and 93 at Lolo, Montana just east of the Wild and Scenic River Corridor. If done instead of the US 12 routing, it adds about 140 miles to the main route. If this is a fly-drive trip originating in Spokane, it's a wise alternative, adding less than a hundred miles to the itinerary. We'll pick up the route from Lewiston, although many readers might find it more convenient to join at Coeur d'Alene. Since the route is still a loop even with this alternative, it doesn't matter how you approach it.

Traveling north on US 95 from Lewiston it's 23 miles to the town of Moscow. Home of the **University of Idaho**, Moscow is an attractive college town. Lodging choices abound. The University is a prime center for agricultural research, development and training. Campus museums feature exhibits as diverse as paleontology and mounted big game trophies. The Shattuck Arboretum of hardwood trees is also on the sprawling campus located in the southwest quadrant of the town. Moscow's premier tourist attraction, though, is just west of town on the Washington state line along SR 8. The **Appaloosa Horse Club** contains many interesting exhibits related to the Nez Perce Indians, but is best known for its large collection of items on the Appaloosa breed of horse. The Nez Perce were and remain famous for both breeding the Appaloosa and for their skilled horsemanship. Allow at least 30 minutes for the Club.

From Moscow, US 95 travels close to the Washington line, an attractive stretch of some 85 miles through the forest and mountains before reaching one of the state's best known resort areas – Coeur d'Alene, metropolis of the Panhandle. The unusual name was given to the area by French fur traders and means "heart of the awl." It's believed that the name refers to the tough negotiating policy of the Nez Perce, who only reluctantly permitted the early traders to operate in the area. Once primarily a mill town, Coeur d'Alene now churns out happy tourists and vacationers. The town is located on the large lake of the same name.

Coeur d'Alene Lake is considered by many people to be one of the world's most beautiful and we won't find any fault with that assessment. It's 25 miles long and averages two to three miles across. Every possible kind of water sport can be found along its shore, but a popular pastime for visitors is a two-hour cruise on the lake. Cruises depart from the city dock at the foot of Independence Point. The Point, itself an attractive area, is reached by descending the steps in City Park that go down to the very edge of the water.

The **Coeur d'Alene Resort** is the town's most famous place to stay, known for its ideal location on the lake front and unusual architecture featuring many peaked roofs. The Resort also boasts the "world's longest" floating boardwalk, running for approximately 3,500 feet. The boardwalk provides magnificent views of the mountains and forest rimming the lake and you'll honestly be able to tell your friends that you walked on water during your visit to Coeur d'Alene!

The **Museum of Northern Idaho** (located on Northwest Blvd. in the heart of downtown) is devoted to the area's mining and logging heritage, with additional exhibits on transportation and the early settlers. It's one of the larger museums of its type in the state and requires a minimum of 45 minutes to fully explore.

Another attraction that might be of interest if you're traveling with children or just need a break from sightseeing is **Wild Waters** on Government Way off of I-90, Exit 12. The park has several water slides and other water-related recreational pursuits.

Coeur d'Alene has accommodations ranging from the simple to the luxurious. Although you may not choose to stay at the Coeur d'Alene Resort (but be sure not to miss it even if you stay elsewhere), you'll find many of the major chains, including Best Western, Choice, Fairfield Inn and Holiday Inn.

Upon leaving Coeur d'Alene, your journey will continue north on US 95. But there are a few more attractions within a short distance of the town. The first is only six miles north. The **Aerial Retardant Plant** processes the chemicals used to fight forest fires from aerial tankers. During the summer interesting hour-long tours of the plant are given. Although we certainly hope that you don't encounter any forest fires during your travels, if there happens to be one in progress, visitors are allowed to observe the process of loading the tankers with fire-fighting chemicals. Continuing for another nine miles, you'll reach **Silverwood**. This is a recreation of a frontier town, done in an ornate Victorian architectural style. The "town" features everything from thrill rides that children will love to a more sedate train ride into the surrounding woodlands – sedate that is until you're suddenly "attacked" by robbers and have to survive an intense gunfight. Silverwood is fun for all ages and if amusement parks with a touch of history are your thing, you could find yourself spending four or more hours here.

Okay, so by now you've probably had enough of US 95. You'll see the last of it about a half-hour north of Silverwood upon reaching the town of Sandpoint. This is another very picturesque community, located on the north end of **Pend Oreille Lake**. One of the Panhandle's many star water attractions, this lake is of glacial origin. It is 1,150 feet deep. Like Coeur d'Alene Lake, it provides opportunities for every type of water sport. Even if you don't partake in such sporting activities, do be sure to visit the lake itself, as it certainly doesn't give much away in beauty to its more famous neighbor to the south. In the town of Sandpoint is the **Bonner County Historical Museum** (Ontario Street on the lake front) and the **Vintage Wheels Museum**. While the former is pretty much standard local history fare, Vintage Wheels is unusual for this part of the country. It has a fine collection of antique cars (including a Stanley Steamer), as well as horse-drawn vehicles. Allow a minimum of 45 minutes to visit the car museum.

A very popular activity in Sandpoint is to take one of the surprisingly inexpensive rides on a horse-drawn trolley through the downtown area. While the trolley was once upon a time considered to be the solution to the town's increasing traffic, it has been retained primarily for the benefit of visitors. It's relaxing and fun, as well as a good way to see the city. While you're downtown, also allow some time to browse the shops at the **Cedar Street Bridge Public Market**. This once was a municipal bridge but has since been transformed into an unusual and attractive mall, with a two-story plaza. Many of Sandpoint's best restaurants are located here. Lodging is also available in Sandpoint.

Leave Sandpoint heading east on SR 200. The road runs along the north shore of Pend Oreille Lake. At Clark's Fork is the **Cabinet Gorge Dam**. There is a lookout point which gives you a great view of the scenic setting. A fish hatchery is also located in the complex. A couple of miles past the dam you'll reach the Montana border, with Idaho 200 becoming Montana 200.

The stretch on SR 200 in Montana runs through the Cabinet Mountains and the Kootenai National Forest, so the ride is scenic and pleasant, although it's rather long. Therefore, it would be a good idea to spend the previous night in Sandpoint, since the small communities along SR 200 don't have a very good selection of places to stay. SR 200 runs into US 93 just north of Missoula. (Attractions in the Missoula area were described in the Montana chapter). Take US 93 southbound and a few miles south of Missoula you'll reach Lolo, where you rejoin the main itinerary.

The Teton Valley Circle

This extended loop off of the main route at Idaho Falls adds a significant amount of mileage and time to the trip. But the highlight is Yellowstone National Park and it is included here for those visitors who will not otherwise be visiting Wyoming.

From Idaho Falls, head towards Rexburg on US 20. The road markers will say east, but you're actually traveling north at this point. About 30 miles north of Idaho Falls is Rexburg. In town is the **Teton Flood Museum** which chronicles the 1976 disaster resulting from the collapse of the Teton Dam. Then resume your journey on US 20. This road is on the western side of the Teton Mountains in an area known as the Teton Valley. You'll have an unobstructed view of the west slopes of the Tetons, a view not seen from within Grand Teton National Park itself.

One further attraction accessible by US 20 is the **St. Anthony Sand Dunes**, located near the town of St. Anthony, just a few miles north of Rexburg. The dunes, which are quite unexpected in this part of the country, cover about 15 square miles. The Bureau of Land Management has an information center to make your visit more meaningful.

US 20 will take you into Montana and the town of West Yellowstone, one of the major gateways to Yellowstone National Park. The town boasts a population of less than a thousand people, but is always bustling with visitors in summer. Western-style architecture lends an almost theme-park atmosphere to "downtown." The **Museum of the Yellowstone** is located in a former Union Pacific train depot and houses extensive displays on area wildlife and the people who have lived and worked in the region, from native Americans to the cavalry. You can also get a preview of your visit to the park with some of the Yellowstone National Park exhibits. Give yourself about 40 minutes to visit the museum.

Having come this far to get to Yellowstone, you should first take a detour 17 miles northwest of town via scenic route US 287 to the fascinating and beautiful **Madison River Canyon Earthquake Area**. A catastrophic earthquake in 1959 rearranged the landscape by blocking a river as well as tossing huge boulders around like toys and slanting the bottom of a large lake. The area today encompasses almost 40,000 acres and includes lovely Lakes Hegben and Earthquake. You'll still see much evidence of the damage from an observation room. A separate exhibit tells the story of some of North America's most famous earthquakes. Give yourself about an hour to tour the area.

From here, refer to the section in the Wyoming chapter on both Yellowstone and Grand Teton National Parks, as well as the Jackson Hole area. Upon leaving Jackson, pick up SR 32 and 33 west, which will soon return you to Idaho, traveling through the lovely

Targhee National Forest. At the junction of SR 31 take that road for 21 miles to Swan Valley and then west on US 26, which takes you back to Idaho Falls.

Excluding the mileage within the National Parks, the round trip to the two parks from Idaho Falls covers about 205 miles, certainly worth your time to see two of America's most stunning natural wonders.

Other Short Side Trips

The remainder of the routes described below are all relatively short spurs leading off of and returning to the main itinerary from the same point or close to it. How many you do depends upon your interests and available time.

Idaho City

This 80-mile round-trip excursion from Boise takes you to the historic town and once pretender as the state capital of Idaho City. The trip is entirely via SR 21, a most beautiful road known as the **Ponderosa Pine Scenic Route**. It travels through the Boise National Forest amid heavily wooded mountain slopes. The route beyond Idaho City is also scenic, going all the way to the Sawtooth National Recreation Area.

Developed as a mining town in 1862, the silver boom once made Idaho City one of the Pacific Northwest's largest cities, with the population at one point rising to over 30,000 people. Today, about 300 make it their full time home, although Boisians frequent it in droves on summer weekends. There are many historic buildings still remaining that you can discover on a walk around town, including the Masonic Hall and old territorial prison. Allow about five hours for this side trip.

Idaho's Ghost Towns

This is a 130-mile round trip, much of it on unpaved roads. While some of them are a little difficult, they are not of the type that require four-wheel drive or high clearance. From Nampa head south about 28 miles via SRs 45 and 78 to Murphy and then via an unpaved road to **DeLamer** and beyond to **Silver City**. These once prosperous mining towns have seen better days. DeLamer is a true ghost town, having no inhabitants today, while Silver City is all but officially a ghost town. The eerie feeling in these towns of decaying buildings is made even more so by the surrounding desolate mountains. The Owyhee Mountain range has some impressive scenery and you'll be crossing the New York Summit at an elevation of 6,676 feet. There are few facilities along the entire route, which should take five hours to complete, so eat and fill up the gas tank in Nampa.

To the Springs

Our next suggested diversion is a 120-mile round trip, leaving the main route from and returning to Pocatello. Take I-15 south to the Mt. Cammon exit and head east on US 30 to the town of Lava Hot Springs. The springs, with water gushing out at a constant temperature of 110 degrees, have made it a popular health and recreation resort. The **South Bannock County Historical Center** is a museum which traces the area's importance as a part of the Oregon Trail, but the main attraction in town is the **Idaho Famous Hot Pools and Olympic Complex**. Mineral baths in natural pools are available at modest cost to those who might be tempted by the beneficial effects of the waters. There is also an outdoor Olympic-size swimming pool that is open to the public. The area is worth a visit even if you aren't going to take to the water because of the attractive gardens that have been built into terraces on the side of a small extinct volcano.

About 20 miles further east from Lava Hot Springs is Soda Springs, so called because of the natural soda water that comes from the ground. Its local nickname is "Beer Springs." You can still sample the soda water today. It's delicious. The area is home to many different mineral springs, giving it a rather eerie appearance. Natural travertine terraces have formed over the years, although not to the extent found at Yellowstone National Park. There is a geyser here as well – Captive Geyser erupts hourly. The name was given because the geyser has been made captive through control of its eruptions (wind conditions permitting).

At least a half-day should be allowed for the Springs side trip, with a full day more recommended if you're going swimming or taking mineral baths. Overnight accommodations are available in both Lava Hot Springs and Soda Springs.

The City of Rocks

This 90-mile round trip originates near Burley. Take Exit 216 off of I-84. The easiest route is on SR 27 and SR 77 via Albion and Elba, then following signs for Almo before picking up an unpaved road for four miles west to the **Silent City of Rocks**. (A shorter route is available by staying on SR 27 to Oakley and then 18 miles by unpaved roads to the City of Rocks. However, this route is often difficult to negotiate and the longer method is preferable unless you have a high-clearance, four-wheel drive vehicle.)

This attraction gets its name from settlers on the Oregon Trail who thought that the thousands of rocks looked like some ancient civilization. Over two and a half billion years of erosion has transformed most of the rocks into unusual shapes, many with fanciful names such as the Devil's Bedstead and the Giant Toad-stool. Some of the formations are up to 700 feet tall. It's an impressive sight. Only recently have government authorities begun to develop the area so that it will be more accessible to visitors. Given current conditions you should allow almost four hours for the round trip from the Interstate highway.

Bruneau Canyon

This final side excursion also is intended for those who don't mind roughing it a bit as the roads encountered here are, again, not the easiest to drive on. This trip covers about 100 miles, leaving I-84 at the town of Hammett (Exit 112) and returning to I-84 near Mountain Home, 17 miles further west at Exit 95. (If you take this loop you don't miss anything on the main route.) From I-84 take SR 78, which later joins SR 51, toward Bruneau.

Shortly before the town you'll reach **Bruneau Dunes State Park.** The dunes climb to almost 500 feet in some places, making them among the highest in North America. Many visitors climb on the dunes and you might even see some attempting to ski on them. A visitor center will explain the conditions that create these odd features. Continue on to the town of Bruneau and then follow the paved road to Bruneau Hot Springs. Beyond that point there is a 15-mile gravel stretch before another three miles of dirt road to the **Bruneau Overlook**. The ride is a little difficult, but the reward is worth it. From the overlook you'll get a fantastic view into the Bruneau Canyon, with 800-foot-high sheer walls. The canyon is a narrow 1,300 feet wide.

Retrace the route to Bruneau and then follow SR 78 along the **C. J. Strike Reservoir**. The dam can be visited and the ride beside the water is an easy and pleasant one. Just beyond the dam at the town of Grand View, head back toward the Interstate via SR 67. This route passes **Mountain Home Air Force Base** and tours can be arranged by contacting the Public Affairs Office in advance at (208) 828-6800.

This final side trip requires about four to five hours, with an additional 90 minutes if you're touring the Air Force Base.

Addendum 1

Itinerary Outlines

Tthis section summarizes the places visited in each of the three suggested state routes and graphically depicts the alternative routings and side trips. This should enable you to get a quick picture of the possibilities and customize your trip in a logical fashion. Use these charts in conjunction with the state maps in each chapter or, better still, with a detailed road map. The main itinerary runs down the center of each chart. Follow the arrows for alternative routes and side trips.

Individual charts following these route planners give suggestions for points where multi-state trip combinations are best linked together and the mileage you'll add to complete those links.

WYOMING

(Including the Black Hills and Badlands of South Dakota)

Alternative Routes	*Main Itinerary*	*Loops & Other Side Trips*
Laramie ⟵—————————	Cheyenne	
Rock Spring →Flaming Gorge	Douglas	
Green River ⟵	Casper	
Kemmerer	Shoshoni ⟵——⟶	Wind River Canyon
Afton	Riverton	Thermopolis
	Dubois	
⟶	Jackson ↘	Lower Wind River Basin
	Grand Teton Natl Park	
	Yellowstone Natl Park	
Greybull ⟵—————————	Cody	
Shell Canyon	Lovell	
	Bighorn Canyon Natl Rec Area	
⟶	Sheridan	
	Buffalo ⟵——⟶	Ten Sleep Canyon
	Gillette	
	Devils Tower Natl Monument	
	Sundance	
	Spearfish [SD]	
	Deadwood [SD]	
(South Dakota Bypass)	Rapid City [SD]	
	Wall [SD]	
	Badlands National Park [SD]	
	Keystone/Mt. Rushmore [SD]	
	Custer [SD]	
	Hot Springs [SD]	
	Mule Creek Jct.	
	Lusk	
	Ft. Laramie/Guernsey	
	Cheyennne	

MONTANA

Alternative Routes	Main Itinerary	Loops & Other Side Trips
	Billings	
Red Lodge	Livingston	
Beartooth Scenic Hwy	Bozeman	
Yellowstone/Grand Teton NPs	Three Forks	
Gardiner	Whitehall	
	Virginia City	
	Butte	
	Anaconda (Lost Creek)	
	Deer Lodge	
	Missoula ⟵⟶ Ninemile Divide	
	Polson	
	Kalispell ⟵⟶ Whitefish (Extension to Eureka and Libby)	
	Glacier Natl Park	
	Waterton Lakes NP [CAN.]	
	East Glacier Park	
	Browning ⟶ Flathead River	
	Choteau	
	Great Falls	
	Helena	
	Townsend	
	Billings ⟵⟶ Pompeys Pillar	
	Hardin	
	Custer Battlefield Natl Mon.	
	Bighorn Canyon Natl Rec Area	
	Billings	

IDAHO

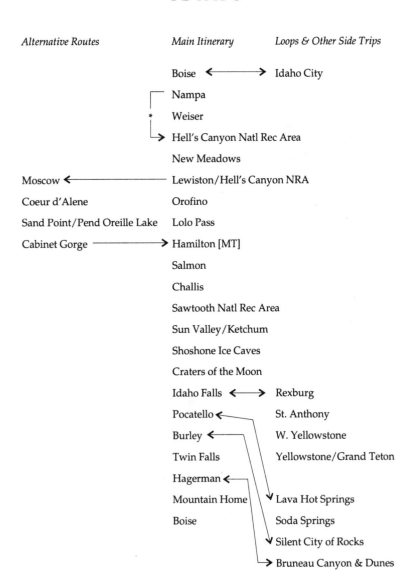

Alternative Routes	Main Itinerary	Loops & Other Side Trips
	Boise ⟷	Idaho City
	Nampa	
*	Weiser	
	Hell's Canyon Natl Rec Area	
	New Meadows	
Moscow ⟵	Lewiston/Hell's Canyon NRA	
Coeur d'Alene	Orofino	
Sand Point/Pend Oreille Lake	Lolo Pass	
Cabinet Gorge ⟶	Hamilton [MT]	
	Salmon	
	Challis	
	Sawtooth Natl Rec Area	
	Sun Valley/Ketchum	
	Shoshone Ice Caves	
	Craters of the Moon	
	Idaho Falls ⟷	Rexburg
	Pocatello ⟵	St. Anthony
	Burley ⟵	W. Yellowstone
	Twin Falls	Yellowstone/Grand Teton
	Hagerman ⟵	
	Mountain Home	Lava Hot Springs
	Boise	Soda Springs
		Silent City of Rocks
		Bruneau Canyon & Dunes

* By-pass this portion of Hell's Canyon (via Oxbow) if you're only going to be visiting the recreation area by boat from Lewiston.

Combining State Itineraries

The states of Wyoming, Montana and Idaho converge at Yellowstone National Park, with the majority of the park being in Wyoming. This makes the northwestern portion of Wyoming the ideal place to link up all or parts of the individual state itineraries. Even if you're not on a trip ambitious enough to cover more than one state, consider using the "Yellowstone option" to see this great wonder of the world. Any combination can also include Grand Teton National Park for just a few extra miles.

CONNECTIONS FROM WYOMING TO/FROM MONTANA:

- ◆ From Mammoth Hot Springs in Yellowstone National Park - North on US 89 via Gardiner to I-90 at Livingston. [Distance: 59 miles]

- ◆ From Tower Junction in Yellowstone National Park -East on US 212 via the Beartooth Scenic Highway to I-90 at Laurel. This is a suggested alternative routing in the Montana chapter. [Distance: 140 miles]

- ◆ From the Madison Junction in Yellowstone National Park - North on US 287 via West Yellowstone and either (a) continuing via 287 to Ennis (near Virginia City, MT) [Distance: 84 miles] or, (b) taking 287 to US 197 and then north on the latter to I-90 at Belgrade. [Distance: 102 miles]

CONNECTIONS FROM WYOMING TO/FROM IDAHO:

- ◆ From the Madison Junction in Yellowstone National Park - North on US 287 to West Yellowstone and then via US 20 (which is the Teton Circle side trip in the Idaho chapter) to Idaho Falls. [Distance: 125 miles]

- ◆ From Jackson at the southern end of Grand Teton National Park - West on Wyoming SR 22 and Idaho SRs 33 and 31 to Idaho Falls. [Distance: 90 miles]

- ◆ If you're on the Wyoming Alternative Route, from Border on US 30 (54 miles past Kemmerer) - Continue West on US 30 to Pocatello. [Distance: 110 miles]

Addendum 2

Quick Reference Attraction Index

This is an alphabetical listing of all attractions, with the page number, hours, and fees.

The hours shown are for the summer months, generally June through September. If traveling at other times of the year it is a good idea to check for closures or reduced hours. When no times are given, the attraction is open all day, at least during daylight hours. Visitor centers in national and state parks are usually open from 8:00 or 9:00 a.m. until at least 5:00 p.m., although the parks themselves do not close or have much longer hours.

PRICES: The figure given indicates the full adult admission price, rounded up to the next dollar, based on prices at time of publication. Thus, these figures are for reference purposes only. Discounts for children or senior citizens are usually available. National and state parks generally do not have a per person admission price, but there is a fee for each car entering. This is waived in the case of national parks for persons who present a Golden Eagle or Golden Age Passport. Areas implememting this fee structure are indicated by a dollar sign ($) in the listing without a specific amount. The letter "D" indicates donations in lieu of a fixed admission price.

WYOMING

Attraction	Hours	Cost	Page
Abraham Lincoln Mem. Mon.		Free	35
Amax Coal Co.	Mon-Fri 8 & 11	Free	24
Ayres Natural Bridge	Daily 8-8	Free	12
Bighorn Canyon		Free	22
Natl Rec. Area			
Boyson Reservoir		Free	37
Bradford Binton Mem. Msm.	Daily 9:30-5	3	24
& Historic Ranch			
Buffalo Bill Hist. Center	Daily 7am-10pm	7	22
Carbon County Museum	Mon-Fri 1-4 & 7-9	Free	36
Carousel Park	Daily 11-10	1	24
Casper Mountain Park		Free	12
Cheyenne Fontier Days	Last full week in July	Varies	10
Cheyenne Frontier Days Old West	Mon-Fri 8-6; Sat-Sun 10-5	3	11
Museum			
Cheyenne St. Railway Trolley	Daily 10am & 1:30pm	6	11
Cody Nite Rodeo	Daily at 8:30pm	7+	22
Crook County Msm. & Art Gallery	Mon-Fri 9-8	Free	25
Devils Tower Natl Mon.		$	24
Dubois Fish Hatchery	Daily 8-5	Free	14
Dubois Museum	Mon-Sat 8-8; Sun 10-5	Free	14
Fetterman Massacre Mon.		Free	23
Flaming Gorge Natl Rec. Area	Dam tours daily 9-5	Free	39
Fort Caspar Msm.	Mon-Sat 9-7; Sun 12-3	Free	12
Fort Fetterman State Hist. Site	Daily 9-5	Free	11
Fort Laramie Natl Hist. Site	Daily 8-7	2	34
Ft. Phil Kearny State Hist. Site	Daily 8-6	1	24
Fossil Butte National Mon.		Free	36
Grand Teton National Park		$	17
Greybull Museum	Mon-Sat 10-8	Free	37
Greybull Wildlife Museum	Mon-Fri 9-4	2	37
Gros Ventre Slide		Free	17
Guernsey State Park Museum	Daily 10-6	$	34
Hell's Half Acre		Free	12
Historic Governors	Tue-Sat 9-5	Free	10
Mansion State His. Site			
Historic Sheridan Inn	Mon-Sat 9-8; Sun 10-4	3	23
Hot Springs State Park	Daily 6am-10pm	Free	38
Jackson Hole Aerial Tram	Daily 8-7	14	16
Jackson Hole Museum	Mon-Sat 9-5:30; Sun 1-4	2	16
Jim Gatchell Mem. Museum	Daily 9-8	2	24
Laramie Peak Museum	Mon-Fri 1-5	Free	11
Laramie Plains Museum	Mon-Sat 9-7; Sun 1-4	4	35
Lincoln County Daughters of	Mon-Fri 1-5	Free	36
Utah Pioneer Msm.			
Medicine Wheel		Free	23
Natl Bighorn Sheep Interpretive Ctr.	Daily 9-8	2	14
National Elk Refuge		Free	16
Occidental House	Daily 11-8	D	24
Oregon Trail Ruts State Hist. Site		Free	34
Periodic Spring		Free	36

Attraction	Hours	Cost	Page
Register Cliff State Historic Site		Free	34
Riverton Museum	Mon-Sat 10-5; Sun 1-4	Free	14
Rockpile Museum	Tue-Sat 9-8; Sun 10-6	Free	24
Ross Berlin's Wildlife Museum	Daily 9-7	2	16
Scenic River Path		Free	11
Shell Canyon & Falls		Free	37
Sinks Canyon State Park		Free	38
Snow King Scenic Chairlift & Alpine Slide	Daily 9-6; Slide 10-8	5 Each	16
South Pass City	Daily 9-5:30	$	38
Stagecoach Museum	Daily 1-5 & 7-9	1	34
Table Rock		Free	36
Ten Sleep Canyon		Free	39
Trail End Hist. Ctr State Hist. Site	Daily 9-5 (Wed till 9pm)	D	23
Trail Town	Daily 8-8	3	22
University of Wyoming	Museum hours vary	Free	35
Wax Museum of Old Wyoming	Daily 9am-10pm	4	16
Wind River Canyon		Free	37
Wyoming Frontier Prison	Daily 8:30-5:30	4	36
Wyoming/Colorado Scenic Railroad	Daily in am. Hours vary	33-50	35
Wyoming Pioneer Mem. Msm.	Mon-Fri 8-7; Sat 1-5	Free	11
Wyoming State Capitol	Mon-Fri 8-4:30	Free	10
Wyoming State Museum	Mon-Fri 8:30-5	Free	10
Wyoming Territorial Park	Daily 9-6	8	35
Yellowstone National Park		$	19

BADLANDS/BLACK HILLS REGION OF
SOUTH DAKOTA

Attraction	Hours	Cost	Page
Badlands National Park		$	30
Bear Country USA	Daily 8am-1 hr. before dusk	8	31
Beautiful Rushmore Cave	Daily 8-8	6	28
Berry Library Learning Center	Mo-Th 7am-11pm; Fri 7-5; Sat 10-5; Sun 2-11	Free	26
Big Thunder Gold Mine	Daily 8-8	6	31
Black Hills Caverns	Daily 8-8	6	28
Black Hills Mining Museum	Daily 9-5	4	26
Black Hills Passion Play	Daily 8-7; Shows Sun, Tue & Th at 8pm	5+	26
Black Hills Reptile Gardens	Daily 7am-8pm	8	30
Broken Boot Gold Mine	Daily 8-6	4	28
Chapel in the Hills	Daily 7am-dusk	D	29
Crazy Horse Memorial		6	33
Crystal Cave Park	Daily 8-8	7	28
Custer State Park		$	32
Dahl Fine Arts Center	Mon-Thu 9-8; Fri-Sat 9-5; Sun 1-5	D	29
1880 Train	Daily; hours vary	13	33
Ellsworth Air Force Base	Daily 8:30-4:30	4	29
Flinstones Bedrock City	Daily 8-8	5	33
Ghosts of Deadwood Gulch/ Western Heritage Msm.	Daily 8-6	4	28
High Plains Heritage Center	Daily 9-5	3	26
Homestake Gold Mine	Mon-Fri 9-5; Sat-Sun 10-5	4	26
Jewel Cave National Park	Daily; varies	8	29
Mammoth Site	Daily 8-8	3	33
Marine Life Aquarium	Daily 8-6	8	30
Mount Moriah Cemetery	Daily 7am-8pm	1	28
Mount Rushmore Natl Memorial	Daily 8am-10pm	Free	31
Museum of Geology	Mon-Sat 8-6; Sun 12-6	Free	29
National Museum of Woodcarving	Daily 8am-8:30pm	6	33
Norbeck Overlook		Free	32
Pactola Reservoir		Free	28
Parade of Presidents Wax Museum	Daily 8:30-6	6	31
Rushmore-Borglum Story	Daily 8-8	5	31
Sitting Bull Crystal Caverns	Daily 7-7	6	28
South Dakota Air & Space Museum	Daily 8:30-6	Free	29
Spearfish Canyon Scenic Highway		Free	26
Stagebarn Crystal Cave	Daily 8-8	5	28
Trial of Jack McCall...Murder of Wild Bill Hickok	Mon-Sat at 8pm	4-5	28
Wall Drug		N/A	29
Wind Cave National Park	Daily 9-6	4-10	33
Wonderland Cave Natural Park	Daily 8am-9pm	6	29

MONTANA

Attraction	Hours	Cost	Page
Adler Gulch Work Train	Daily 10:30-5	4	46
American Computer Museum	Daily 10-4	2	44
Beartooth Scenic Highway		Free	58
Big Mtn Ski & Summer Resort	Daily 9-9	9	60
Big Sky Waterslide	Daily 10-8	4-11	50
Big Timber Waterslide	Daily 10-7	12	42
Bighorn Canyon Natl Rec. Area		Free	57
Billings Night Rodeo	Daily at 8pm	7	42
Carbon County Hist. Museum	Daily 10-6	D	58
Cathedral of St. Helena	Mon-Fri 10-4; Sat 10-6:30; Sun 7-Noon	Free	55
Chief Black Otter Trail		Free	42
C. M. Russell Museum	Mon-Sat 9-6; Sun 1-5	4	53
Conrad Mansion Natl Hist. Site	Daily 9-8	5	50
Copper King Mansion	Daily 9-4	5	46
Daly Mansion (Idaho Tour)	Tue-Sun 11-4	5	75
Deep Creek Canyon Drive		Free	56
Depot Center Museum	Mon-Sat 9-5; Sun 1-5	3	44
Far West Cruise Ship	Daily at 2pm	7	50
Flathead Lake		Free	50
Flathead River Gorge		Free	49
Frontier Gateway Museum	Mon-Sat 9-12 & 1-5; Sun 1-5	D	63
Frontier Town	Daily 10-10	Free	56
Gallatin County Pioneer Museum	Mon-Fri 10-4:30; Sat 1-4	Free	44
Gates of the Mountains Rec. Area	Mon-Fri 11, 1 & 3; Sat 10, 2 & 4; Sun 10-5 (boat tours)	8	54
Giant Springs Fish, Wildlife & Parks Visitor Ctr.		$	54
Gilbert Brewery	Mon, Wed & Sun evenings	8	45
Glacier Maze	Daily 9-6	5	50
Glacier National Park		$	51
Grand Menard Discovery Trails		Free	60
Grant-Kohrs Ranch Natl Hist. Site	Daily 9-5:30	$	48
Historic Museum at Fort Missoula	Tue-Sat 10-5; Sun 12-5	D	48
Hungry Horse Dam	Daily 9:30-6	Free	50
Last Chance Gulch Tour	Daily 8:30-6:30	4	56
Lewis & Clark Caverns State Park	Daily 9-7	6	45
Little Bighorn Battlefield Natl Mon.	Daily 8-8	$	57
Lone Wolf Wildlife Museum	Daily 9-6	3	44
Lost Creek State Park		$	47
Madison Buffalo Jump State Hist. Site		$	45
Madison River Canyon Earthquake Area (Idaho Tour)	Daily 9-6	D	86
Makoshika State Park		$	63
Malstrom Air Force Base Museum & Air Park	Mon-Sat 12-3	Free	54
Mineral Museum	Daily 8-5	Free	46
Miracle of America Museum	Mon-Sat 8-5; Sun 2-6	2	50
Missouri Headwaters State Park		$	44
Montana Hist. Society Msm., Library & Archives	Mon-Fri 8-6; Sat-Sun 8-5	D	55

Attraction	Hours	Cost	Page
Montana State Capitol	Mon-Sat 10-4; Sun 11-3	Free	55
Moss Mansion	Mon-Sat 10-5; Sun 1-3	5	42
Museum of the Plains Indians	Daily 9-5	Free	53
Museum of the Rockies	Daily 9-5	5	44
Museum of the Yellowstone (Idaho Tour)	Daily 8am-10pm	4	86
National Bison Range		Free	49
Ninemile Remount Depot & Ranger Station	Daily 8-4:30	D	60
Ninepipe National Wildlife Refuge		Free	49
Old Montana Prison	Daily 8am-9pm	5	47
Old Number 1	Daily 10:30, 1:30, 3:30 & 7	4	46
Old Trail Museum	Daily 9-6	D	53
Original Governor's Mansion	Tue-Sun 12-4	Free	55
Our Lady of the Rockies	Daily at 10 & 2	10	47
Oscar's Dreamland	Daily 9-6	5	42
Park County Museum	Daily 12-5 & 7-9	2	44
Peter Yegen Jr. Yellowstone County Museum	Mon-Fri 10:30-5:30; Sun 2-5	D	42
Pictographs Cave State Monument		$	57
Polson-Flathead Hist. Museum	Mon-Sat 9-6; Sun 12-6	D	50
Pompeys Pillar Natl. His. Lewis & Clark Landmark	Daily 9-6	Free	59
Port Polson Princess	Daily; departures vary	10-16	50
Prairie County Museum	Mon, Wed-Fri 9-3; Sat-Sun 1-4	Free	63
Range Rider of the Yellowstone		Free	42
Range Riders Museum & Bert Clark Gun Collection	Daily 8-8	4	63
Reeders Alley		Free	56
Rocky Mountain Elk Foundation & Wildlife Vis. Center	Daily 9-7	D	48
St. Francis Xavier Church	Mon-Sat 9-4:30	Free	48
St. Ignatius Mission	Daily 9-9	D	49
Smokejumpers Base Aerial Fire Dep.	Daily 9-5	D	48
Snowbowl Ski Area	Fri-Sun 12-5	6	49
Spencer Watkins Mem. Museum	Daily 9-6	D	45
Towe Ford Museum	Daily 8am-9pm	5	47
Ulm Pushkin State Monument		$	54
Virginia City		Varies	45
Virginia City Opera House	Tue-Fri & Sun at 8pm	10	45
Waterton Lakes National Park [Alberta, CANADA]		$	52
Western Heritage Center	Tue-Sat 10-5; Sun 1-5	D	42
World Msm. of Mining & Hell-Roarin' Gulch	Daily 9-9	Free	46
Yellowstone Wildlife Museum	Daily 9-7	2	59
Yesterday's Playthings Doll & Toy Museum	Daily 10-6	2	47

IDAHO

Attraction	Hours	Cost	Page
Aerial Retardant Plant	Daily 7:30-6	Free	84
Appaloosa Horse Club	Mon-Fri 8-5	Free	83
Balanced Rock		Free	81
Bannock County Hist. Museum	Daily 10-6	1	79
Boise Art Museum	Tue-Fri 10-5; Sat-Sun 12-5	3	67
Boise-Cascade Corporation	Mon-Sat 8-5	Free	67
Boise Interagency Fire Center	By reservation	Free	69
Boise State University		Free	68
Boise Tour Train	Daily; hours vary	5	67
Bonner County Historical Museum	Tue-Sat 10-4	1	84
Bonneville Museum	Mon-Fri 10-5; Sat 1-5	1	79
Bruneau Dunes State Park		$	89
Bruneau Overlook		Free	89
Cabinet Gorge Dam		Free	85
Canyon County Historical Museum	Mon-Sat 9-5	Free	70
Cassia County Historical Museum	Tue-Sat 10-5	D	80
Cedar St. Bridge Market Store	Hours vary	N/A	85
C. J. Strike Reservoir		Free	90
Coer d'Alene Lake	Boat tour times vary	Varies	83
Coer d'Alene Resort		Free	83
Craters of the Moon Natl Mon.		$	77
Deer Flat National Wildlife Refuge		Free	69
Discovery Center of Idaho	Tue-Sat 10-5; Sun 12-5	3	67
Dworshak Dam	Daily 10-6	Free	74
Dworshak National Fish Hatchery	Daily 7:30-4	Free	74
Ernest Hemingway Memorial		Free	77
Experimental Breeder Reactor # 1	Daily 8-4	Free	78
First United Methodist Church	Mon-Fri 8:30-5:30	Free	66
Fort Hall Replica	Daily 9-7	1	79
Hagerman Fossil Beds Natl Landmark		Free	81
Heart of the Monster		Free	74
Hells Canyon Natl Rec. Area	Boat tour times vary	Free	73
		(tours 25-70)	
Idaho Botanical Gardens	Tue-Sun 10-5	2	68
Idaho Falls		Free	79
Idaho Falls Zoo	Daily 10-5	4	79
Idaho Famous Hot Pools & Olympic Complex	Daily 8am-11pm	4+	88
Idaho Historical Museum	Mon-Sat 9-5; Sun 1-5	Free	67
Idaho Museum of Natural History	Mon-Sat 9-5; Sun 1-5	3	79
Idaho State Capitol	Mon-Fri 8-5	Free	66
Idaho Transportation Museum	Tue-Sun 10-5	3	68
Julia Davis Park		Free	67
Lehmi County Historical Museum	Mon-Sat 10-5	D	75
Lewis & Clark Canoe Camp		Free	74
Lewis & Clark Hwy. Wild & Scenic River Corridor		Free	74
Lewis & Clark Interpretive Center		Free	73
Lewiston Levee Parkway		Free	73
Lucky Peak State Park		$	69

Attraction	Hours	Cost	Page
Malad Gorge State Park		Free	81
Massacre Rocks State Park		Free	80
Mormon Temple		Free	79
Morrison Knudsen Nature Center		Free	68
Mountain Home Air Force Base	By reservation	Free	90
Museum of Northern Idaho	Tue-Sun 11-5	2	83
Nez Perce National Historic Park	Daily 8-6	Free	74
Old Idaho Penitentiary	Daily 10-5	3	67
Packer John State Park		Free	72
Packer Meadow		Free	75
Payette County Hist. Soc. Msm.	Mon-Sat 9-5; Sun 1-5	Free	70
Pend Oreille Lake		Free	84
Perrine Memorial Bridge		Free	80
Ponderosa Pine Scenic Route		Free	87
Rapid River Salmon Hatchery		Free	72
St. Anthony Sand Dunes		Free	86
Ste. Chapelle Winery	Mon-Sat 10-5; Sun 12-5	Free	70
Salmon River Scenic Route		Free	75
Sawtooth National Recreation Area		Free	76
Shoshone Falls		Free	80
Shoshone Ice Caves	Daily 8-8	5	77
Silent City of Rocks		$	89
Silverwood	Daily 11-10	14	84
South Bannock Cnty Histl Ctr.	Daily 12-5	D	88
Teton Flood Museum	Mon-Sat 10-5	D	86
Thousand Springs		Free	81
Three Island Crossing State Park		Free	82
University of Idaho	Museum hours vary	Free	82
Veterans Memorial State Park		Free	69
Vintage Wheels Museum	Mon-Sat 9:30-5:30; Sun 11-5:30	3	85
Wild Waters	Daily 11-7	11	84
Wild Waters Waterslide Theme Park	Daily 11-7	12	69
World Center for Birds of Prey	Inquire for tour times	D	69
Zoo Boise	Daily 10-5	3	67

Addendum 3

General State Information

WYOMING

Wyoming Travel Commission
I-25 at College Drive
Cheyenne WY 82002
(800) 225-5996

SOUTH DAKOTA

Division of Tourism
711 East Wells Avenue
Pierre SD 57501-3369
(800) 843-1930

Black Hills, Badlands Association
900 Jackson Blvd.
Rapid City SD 57702
(605) 341-1462

MONTANA

Montana Travel Promotion Division
Department of Commerce
1424 9th Avenue
Helena MT 59620
(800) 541-1447

IDAHO

Idaho Travel Council
700 W. State Street, 2nd Floor
Boise ID 83720
(800) 635-7820

National Park Service Facilities

Address all written inquiries to the SUPERINTENDENT of the particular facility at the addresses given.

WYOMING

Bighorn Canyon National Recreation Area
Box 458
Fort Smith MT 59035
(406) 666-2412

Devils Tower National Monument
P.O. Box 8
Devils Tower WY 82714
(307) 467-5283

Flaming Gorge National Recreation Area
Box 278
Manila UT 84046
(801) 784-3445

Grand Teton National Park
P.O. Box Drawer 170
Moose WY 83012
(307) 733-2880

Yellowstone National Park
P.O. Box 168
Yellowstone National Park WY 82190
(307) 344-7381

SOUTH DAKOTA

Badlands National Park
P.O. Box 6
Interior SD 57750
(605) 433-5361

Jewel Cave National Monument
RR 1, Box 60 AA
Custer SD 57730
(605) 673-2288

Wind Cave National Park
RR 1
Box 190-WCNP
Hot Springs SD 57747
(605) 745-4600

MONTANA

Bighorn Canyon National Recreation Area
[See WYOMING listings]

Glacier National Park
West Glacier MT 59936
(406) 888-5441

IDAHO

Craters of the Moon National Monument
P.O. Box 29
Arco ID 83213
(208) 527-3257

Hells Canyon National Recreation Area
88401 Highway 82
Enterprise OR 97828
(503) 426-4978

Sawtooth National Recreation Area
Star Route
Ketchum ID 83340
(208) 726-7672

Lodging

Within National Parks

GRAND TETON NATIONAL PARK

Colter Bay Village
P.O. Box 240
Moran WY 83013
(307) 543-2811*

Jackson Lake Lodge
P.O. Box 240
Moran WY 83013
(307) 543-2861*

Jenny Lake Lodge
P.O. Box 240
Moran WY 83013
(307) 733-4647*

Signal Mountain Lodge
P.O. Box 50
Moran WY 83013
(307) 543-2831

* Reservations for all three of these establishments can be made through
the Grand Teton Lodge Company. Their number is (307) 543-2855.

YELLOWSTONE NATIONAL PARK

Canyon Lodge
Canyon Jct.
Yellowstone Park WY 82190
 (307) 242-3900**

Grant Village
Yellowstone Park WY 82190
(307) 344-7311**

Lake Lodge & Cabins
Lake Station, Box 3307
Yellowstone Park WY 82190
(307) 242-3800**

Lake Yellowstone Hotel & Cabins
Lake Station, Box 3307
Yellowstone Park WY 82190
(307) 242-3700**

Mammoth Hot Springs Hotel & Cabins
Mammoth Hot Springs
Yellowstone Park WY 82190
(307) 344-7311**

Old Faithful Inn
West Thumb & Madison
Yellowstone Park WY 82190
(307) 545-4600**

** All reservations for Yellowstone National Park accommodations are handled by the Travel Director, TW Recreational Services Inc., Yellowstone National Park WY 82190. Telephone: (307) 344-7311.

GLACIER NATIONAL PARK

Apgar Village Inn
East Glacier Park MT 59434
(406) 888-5632

Apgar Village Lodge
P.O. Box 398
West Glacier MT 59936
(406) 888-5484

Glacier Park Lodge
State Route 49
East Glacier Park MT 59434
(406) 226-9311

Lake McDonald Lodge
East Glacier Park MT 59434
(406) 226-5551

Many Glacier Hotel
Swiftcurrent Lake
East Glacier Park MT 59434
(406) 732-4411

Rising Sun Motor Inn
Going-to-the-Sun Highway
East Glacier Park MT 59434
(406) 732-5523

Swiftcurrent Motor Inn
East Glacier Park MT 59434
(406) 226-5551

Major Hotel Chains

Toll-Free Reservation & Information Numbers:

Best Western International	(800) 528-1234
Choice Hotels:	
Clarion Hotels	(800) 221-2222
Comfort Inn	(800) 221-2222
EconoLodge	(800) 424-4777
Friendship Inns	(800) 424-4777
Quality Inns	(800) 221-2222
Rodeway Inns	(800) 221-2222
Days Inn	(800) 325-2525
Hilton Hotels	(800) 445-8667
Holiday Inns	(800) 465-4329
Howard Johnson Motor Lodges	(800) 446-4656
La Quinta Motor Inns	(800) 531-5900
Marriott Hotels:	
Courtyard by Marriott	(800) 321-2211
Fairfield Inns	(800) 228-2800
Marriott Hotels & Resorts	(800) 228-9290
Residence Inn by Marriott	(800) 331-3131
Ramada Inns	(800) 228-2828
Sheraton Hotels	(800) 325-3535
Super 8 Motels	(800) 843-1991
TraveLodge	(800) 255-3050

The following lists show the locations of chains with a significant presence in Wyoming, Montana, Idaho and the Black Hills area of South Dakota. If there is more than one property at a location this is indicated by an asterisk (*). South Dakota locations are *only* those within the area described in this book.

BEST WESTERN

Wyoming
Afton, Alpine, Casper, Cody*, Evanston, Gillette, Jackson*, Laramie*, Lusk, Powell, Rawlins, Rock Springs, Sheridan, Sundance, Thermopolis, Wheatland, Worland

South Dakota
Belle Fourche, Custer, Deadwood, Hill City, Hot Springs, Keystone, Lead, Rapid City*, Spearfish, Sturgis, Wall

Montana
Big Sky, Billings, Bozeman*, Butte*, Dillon, Forsyth, Gardiner, Glendive, Great Falls*, Hamilton, Helena, Kalispell, Laurel, Miles City, Missoula, Polson, Red Lodge, West Yellowstone*

Idaho
Boise*, Bonners Ferry, Burley, Coeur d'Alene, Driggs, Idaho Falls*, McCall, Montpelier, Moscow, Mountain Home, Pocatello*, Rexburg, St. Anthony, Sandpoint, Sun Valley/Ketchum*, Twin Falls*, Wallace

CHOICE

Comfort/Sleep Inns

Wyoming
Buffalo, Casper, Cheyenne, Cody, Rawlins, Rock Springs

South Dakota
Hot Springs, Spearfish

Montana
Billings, Bozeman*, Gardiner, Great Falls, Helena, Livingston, Whitefish

Idaho
Boise*, Caldwell, Coeur d'Alene, Idaho Falls, Mountain Home, Pocatello, Twin Falls

Quality

Wyoming
Cheyenne

South Dakota
Rapid City

Montana
Billings, Whitefish

Idaho
Boise, Idaho Falls, Pocatello, Sandpoint

Clarion

Idaho
Ketchum/Sun Valley

Econo Lodge

Wyoming
Buffalo

South Dakota
Rapid City

Montana
Billings, Bozeman, Helena, Missoula

Idaho
Twin Falls

Friendship

Wyoming
Jackson*, Rock Springs

Montana
Kalispell, Miles City

Rodeway

Wyoming
Gillette

Idaho
Boise

DAYS INN

Wyoming
Cheyenne, Gillette, Jackson, Rawlins, Riverton, Rock Springs, Sheridan

South Dakota
Deadwood, Rapid City, Spearfish, Sturgis, Wall

Montana
Billings, Bozeman, Butte, Glendive, Great Falls, Helena, Kalispell, Lolo, Missoula, Polson, West Yellowstone

Idaho
Coeur d'Alene, Pocatello, Rexburg

HOLIDAY INN

Wyoming
Casper, Cheyenne, Cody, Douglas, Gillette, Laramie, Riverton, Rock Springs, Sheridan, Thermopolis

South Dakota
Rapid City*, Spearfish

Montana
Billings, Bozeman, Great Falls, Missoula

Idaho
Boise, Coeur d'Alene, Post Falls

HOWARD JOHNSON

Wyoming
Buffalo, Cheyenne

South Dakota
Rapid City

Montana
Billings

Idaho
Pocatello

MARRIOTT

Fairfield Inn

Wyoming
Cheyenne

South Dakota
Spearfish

Montana
Billings, Bozeman, Great Falls

Idaho
Coeur d'Alene, Boise

Residence Inn

Idaho
Boise

RAMADA

Wyoming
Cheyenne, Gillette

South Dakota
Rapid City

Montana
Billings

Idaho
Boise, Lewiston

SUPER 8

Wyoming
Buffalo, Casper, Cheyenne, Cody, Douglas, Dubois, Evanston, Gillette, Green River, Jackson, Laramie, Lovell, Powell, Rawlins, Riverton, Sheridan, Torrington, Worland

South Dakota
Belle Fourche, Custer, Deadwood, Hill City, Hot Springs, Rapid City*, Spearfish, Sturgis, Wall

Montana
Belgrade, Big Timber, Billings, Bozeman, Butte, Columbus, Conrad, Dear Lodge, Dillon, Gardiner, Glendive, Great Falls, Hamilton, Hardin, Havre, Helena, Kalispell, Lewistown, Libby, Livingston, Miles City, Missoula*, Polson, Red Lodge, St. Regis, Swan Valley, West Yellowstone

Idaho
Boise, Coeur d'Alene, Idaho Falls, Kellogg, Lewiston, Moscow, Nampa, Pocatello, Rexburg, Sandpoint, Twin Falls

Major National Car Rental Companies

Alamo	(800) 327-9633
Avis	(800) 321-1212
Budget	(800) 527-0700
Dollar	(800) 421-6868
Enterprise	(800) 325-8007
Hertz	(800) 654-3131
National	(800) 227-7368
Thrifty	(800) 367-2277

Other Information

Since whitewater, float and other outdoor adventures are such an integral part of any vacation in the Northern Rockies, the following operators are listed for your convenience:

WYOMING

Cody
River Runners Boat Trips
(800) 535-RAFT
1½ to 6 hours; whitewater

Wyoming River Trips
(800) 586-6661
3-6 hours; scenic float & whitewater

Jackson/Grand Teton
Barker-Ewing
(800) 365-1800
2+ hours; scenic float trips

Barker-Ewing
(800) 448-4202
Half-day & overnight; whitewater

Charles Sands Wild Water
(800) 358-8184
Full day & overnight; whitewater

Dave Hansen River Trips
(307) 733-6295
Half- & full-day whitewater or combination float and whitewater

Fort Jackson Float Trips
(800) 735-8430
Full-day scenic float trips

Grand Teton Lodge Co.
(307) 543-2855
3 hours; scenic float trips

Jackson Hole Whitewater
(800) 648-2602
3 hours; whitewater

Lewis & Clark Expeditions
(800) 824-5375
2+ hours; whitewater

Lone Eagle Expeditions
(800) 321-3800
3 hour/half-day; whitewater

Mad River Boat Trips
(800) 458-RAFT
1½-3 hour; whitewater

National Park Float Trips
(Triangle X Float Trips)
(307) 733-5500
2+ hours; scenic float trips

Osprey Snake River Trips
(307) 733-5500
As above, but in different direction

Snake River Park Whitewater
(307) 733-7078
2 hour; whitewater

Solitude Float Trips
(307) 733-2871
1½-3 hours; scenic float trips

MONTANA

Polson
Glacier Raft Company
(800) 654-4359
Half-day; whitewater

West Glacier
Glacier Raft Company
(800) 332-9995
Half-day to multi-day; whitewater

Great Northern Whitewater
(800) 735-7897
Half-day to multi-day; whitewater

Montana Rafting Company
(800) 521-RAFT
Half-day to multi-day; whitewater

Wild River Adventure
(800) 826-2724
Half-day to multi-day; whitewater

IDAHO

Hells Canyon from Lewiston
Beamers
(800) 522-6966
Jet-boat excursion

Snake River Adventures
(800) 746 3568
Jet-boat excursion

Hells Canyon from Oxbow, OR
Hells Canyon Adventures
(800) 422-3568
Jet-boat excursion

All of the above Hells Canyon operators also offer excursions by
non-power boat. These range from one to seven days in length.
For additional operators contact the Lewiston Chamber of Commerce at (208) 743-3531

In the case of float and/or whitewater trips, all operators provide experienced guides (although some offer combination guide/self-paddle trips). Protective clothing is provided. Leave photographic equipment behind unless you have water-proof covers that fully enclose the camera. Transportation from the operator's office to the launch site is included. Reservations are often required, but are strongly recommended in all cases. Please note that the toll-free numbers are sometimes only for calls from out of state. If you're calling locally inquire as to the local number.

WAGON TRAIN TRIPS

Teton Country Prarie Schooner
Box 2140
Jackson, WY 83001
(800) 772-5386.
3 nights, covering Grand Teton and Yellowstone National Parks.

Wagons West
Box 1156 Afton, WY 83110
(800) 447-4711
1 to 5 nights, covering the Tetons and the valley of Jackson Hole.

Trails West
65 Main Street
South Pass City, WY 83110
(800) 327-4052
1 or 2 nights, covering the Lower Wind River Basin.

Additional Reading
from Hunter Publishing

ARIZONA, COLORADO & UTAH: A TOURING GUIDE
$11.95, ISBN 1-55650-667-8, 416pp
Larry H. Ludmer

A compact guide written for those eager to see the unforgettable sights and attractions in these three states. Driving tours begin in the state capital and cover the museums, parks, zoos, and historical buildings in each city. They then lead you out into the fascinating land of giant arches, pinnacles, canyons, and deserts for which the region is so well known. All the sights are described, along with maps that show the best routes to reach them. Accommodations and restaurants are listed. An attraction index gives opening times and fees for every sight on your journey.

THE GREAT AMERICAN WILDERNESS:
TOURING AMERICA'S NATIONAL PARKS
$11.95, ISBN 1-55650-567-1, 320pp
Larry H. Ludmer

Covering the 41 most scenic parks throughout the US, including Acadia, the Great Smokey Mountains, Yellowstone, Hawaii Volcanoes, Big Bend, and Everglades, this guide tells you where to stay, where to eat, which roads are the most crowded or the most beautiful, how much time to allow, what you can safely skip and what you must not miss. Detailed maps of each park show all access routes. Special sections help you make the most of your time if you only have a couple of hours.

CANADIAN ROCKIES ACCESS GUIDE 3rd Edition
$15.95, ISBN 0-91943-392-8, 369pp
John Dodd $ Gail Helgason

The ultimate guide to outdoor adventure from Banff to Lake Louise to Jasper National Park. Walking, canoeing routes, climbs, cycling, and hiking in one of the most spectacular regions on earth. Maps, photos and contact numbers make this book an invaluable tool for those seeking to explore nature at its best.

ADVENTURE GUIDE TO THE HIGH SOUTHWEST
$14.95, ISBN 1-55650-633-3, 384pp
Steve Cohen

"Cohen's book is exhaustive in its detail, concern for your safety, the protection of the culture and environment, and compelling in its descriptions." Quick Trips.

Hiking, mountaineering, trail riding, cycling, camping, river running, ski touring, wilderness trips – this book has it all! It is the most adventurous guide to enjoying the natural attractions of the Four Corners area of Northwest New Mexico, Southwest Colorado, Southern Utah, Northern Arizona, and the Navajo Nation and Hopiland. Includes all practical details on transportation, services, where to eat and sleep, plus valuable travel tips on how to cope with the harsh terrain and climate.

THE ADVENTURE GUIDE TO THE CATSKILLS AND ADIRONDACKS
$9.95, ISBN 1-55650-681-3, 192pp
Wilbur H. Morrison

Less than a day's drive from Boston, New York, or Philadelphia, this region offers wilderness reserves, hundreds of acres of forest land, and some of the best outdoor adventures in the US. Here is the ultimate guide to exploring this beautiful area. Covering history, where to stay, where to eat, hiking trails, campsites, what to see and do in the towns (including walking tours), museums, touring routes, and more.

COASTAL CALIFORNIA - A CAMPING GUIDE
$14.95, ISBN 1-55650-679-1, 224pp
George Cagala

This book is filled with all the information a camper needs. From Imperial Beach on the Mexican border to the secluded banks of Smith River near the northern state line, George Cagala gives you candid evaluations of every campground within five miles of the coast. Security, areas to avoid, facilities offered, and valuable advice makes this the most useful guide on the market today. George Cagala also wrote **HAWAII - A CAMPING GUIDE** ($11.95, ISBN 1-55650-641-4, 160pp) for Hunter Publishing.

WHERE TO STAY IN THE AMERICAN NORTHWEST
$12.95, ISBN 1-55650-683-X, 448pp
Phil Philcox

This exhaustive accommodation resource brings you over 4,000 places to stay in Alaska, Wyoming, Idaho, Montana, Oregon, Washington, and the Dakotas. From a luxury penthouse suite in downtown Seattle to a rustic cottage in the Black Hills of South Dakota. Names, addresses, facilities offered, phone numbers, and prices are listed. A special section covers chain hotels and discount programs they run for educational groups, government workers, and business travellers.

OTHER BOOKS IN THE "WHERE-TO-STAY" SERIES

FLORIDA 2nd Edition	$12.95, 1-55650-682-1, 400pp
AMERICA'S HEARTLAND	$13.95, 1-55650-632-5, 565pp
AMERICA'S EASTERN CITIES	$11.95, 1-55650-600-7, 412pp
AMERICA'S WESTERN CITIES	$11.95, 1-55650-601-5, 412pp
AMERICAN SOUTHEAST	$12.95, 1-55650-651-1, 512pp
AMERICAN SOUTHWEST	$12.95, 1-55650-625-X, 448pp
MID-ATLANTIC STATES	$12.95, 1-55650-631-7, 448pp
NORTHERN CALIFORNIA	$12.95, 1-55650-572-8, 280pp
SOUTHERN CALIFORNIA	$12.95, 1-55650-573-6, 380pp
NEW ENGLAND	$11.95, 1-55650-602-3, 500pp

THE BEST PLACES TO STAY IN SOUTH AMERICA VOL I
Colombia, Ecuador, Peru, Bolivia, & Chile
$14.95, ISBN 1-55650-696-1, 288pp
Alex Newton

The first in a unique pair of guides to the top places to bed down for the night in these five countries. Intimate inns, hidden resorts, 200-year-old haciendas, and family-run Bed & Breakfasts are recommended for their atmosphere, their location, and what they have to offer. Profiles are based on personal visits by the author. Volume II covers the eastern half of the continent, including Brazil, Argentina and Venezuela.

For a free copy of our color catalog, please call (908) 225 1900.